In It Together

THE BEAUTIFUL STRUGGLE UNITING US ALL

━━━ ECKHART AURELIUS HUGHES ━━━

In It Together: The Beautiful Struggle Uniting Us All

by Eckhart Aurelius Hughes

Published by OnlineBookClub.org

Manchester, Connecticut, USA

Copyright © 2022 OnlineBookClub.org

LCCN:

2022914477

ISBNs:

978-1-948472-02-9 (hardcover)

978-1-948472-03-6 (paperback)

978-1-948472-04-3 (ebook)

Table of Contents

Dedication

To my kids, my son Tristen and my daughter Amaya.

I love you, always.

If I could sing or play an instrument for you, I would sing and play an instrument for you.

If I could dance for you, I would dance for you.

If I could paint for you, I would paint for you.

But my thing is words.

The problem about words is you may listen to them, and that would be a mistake. For all I am doing is painting with words, and the message that is being sent is non-verbal.

For, in fact, I am not going to say anything that you don't know already.

The perplexing problem is, you don't know you know.

Chuang Tzu says, "The fish trap exists because of the fish. Once you've gotten the fish, you can forget the trap. The rabbit snare exists because of the rabbit. Once you've got the rabbit, you can forget the snare. Words exist because of meaning. Once you've gotten the meaning, you can forget the words. Where can I find a man who has forgotten words, so I can have a word with him?"

You don't have to try; you don't even have to listen. We just have to BE together.

Opening Letter: A force of unbelievable love and goodness...

Dear Friend,

I believe there is a force of unbelievable love and goodness deep within you, and that force is you more than anything is you. It's like a beautiful light trying to work its way out of you, and shine through your art or shine through your deepest feelings of love and through your kindness.

Sometimes the world seems so dark and lonely, no matter how bright the sun shines or how many people you find within your physical vicinity.

Sometimes you may feel lost in the world. Sometimes you may feel the world has lost sight of you.

But more of us see the light in you than you realize. If we fail to show it to you sometimes, or most of the time, maybe it's because we are trapped in the dark trying to get out too.

Stay strong, my friend. There's beauty in the struggle. There's so much to overcome, but imagine what it could mean to overcome it. You are truly amazing, even if it often goes unseen or unshown. The world only seems so cold and dark sometimes because you are so bright. Your incredible potential sets a high bar.

If you went to sleep in your body in your bed with your memories, and awoke in my body in my bed with my memories, would you notice a difference? Would there even be a difference to notice?

INTRODUCTION
—— *A Common Struggle* ——

My favorite writer, Voltairine de Cleyre, died over a century ago, in 1912.

Like the words of many other great minds throughout human history and to this day who have also spoken of fundamental human equality and freedom, Voltairine's heartfelt words cultivated anger or even ridicule in most of those who heard her words of love and freedom.

Love, equality, freedom, and peace may be the most dangerously controversial subjects about which one can speak. To speak in support of love, one challenges haters. To speak in support of fundamental human equality, one challenges sexists, racists, and those who would dehumanize others as inferior. To speak of freedom and peace, one challenges violent oppressors; one challenges murderers, rapists, and enslavers, the most dangerous of whom may be the ones who claim to commit such violence for the alleged greater good.

Such self-proclaimed utilitarians may be the most dangerous people, if not for their self-righteousness, then for the eager willingness with which they commit violent atrocities. Indeed, the most dangerous people capable of the most violent acts often tend to be the ones who think they, unequally, are the so-called "good guys".

Despite living in a time and place where marital rape was legal, which was the USA only a little over a century ago, Voltairine, in the name of peace and equal freedom for all, suggested that women *not* be

1

treated as property or sex slaves, but rather as political equals to men. For many in her time, to suggest such a thing was to suggest laughable chaos. To suggest women be treated as equal to men was to suggest chaos. To suggest giving women the right to vote—let alone merely the right to not be legally raped by their husbands—was to suggest chaos, upheaval, and absurdity. Legal violence, including literal legal rape, in which one person or group violently dominates another, was considered order, and the idea of peace and freedom—*the idea that, since we are fundamentally equals, none of us has a right to violently dominate the other*—was absurd chaos.

In Voltairine's time, merely about one hundred years ago, to suggest that black people be treated as equal to whites, not merely as say three-fifths, was considered absurd by many.

It was to be a rabble-rouser.

It was considered chaos-inducing rabble-rousing to suggest that there be political equality for all people rather than two classes of human beings: oppressor and oppressed, supremacist and perceived inferior, oligarch and peasant, patriarch and slave.

Voltairine died eight years before women would be granted the right to vote in the USA. She died many decades before Dr. Martin Luther King Jr. would march the streets of the United States, repeatedly get arrested, and eventually become assassinated for his similarly controversial message of love, peace, and human equality.

Like Voltairine, when Dr. Martin Luther King Jr. died, he was one of the most hated men in America, hated by establishment politicians on both the left and the right, hated by the wealthy owners of the mainstream media, hated by Democrats, hated by Republicans, hated by the military-industrial complex, and hated by the wealthy special interest groups and paid lobbyists that steered the plutocratic oligarchic government under which he was a despised criminal, a repeatedly arrested repeat offender.

This is not a political book.

The suffering we endure as human beings in this world on this planet spreads out far beyond merely the relatively petty political sphere.

The enslavements and false authorities from which this book seeks to see you liberated exist not merely in the form of other humans and not merely on the relatively small political stage of one tiny planet in a tiny sliver of time in an unfathomably vast universe.

Rather, the political philosophy of political freedom, nonviolence, and self-government acts as an analogue for a much broader and grander spiritual philosophy of spiritual freedom. For instance, the political freedom that is *self-government* acts as an analogue of the much broader spiritual freedom that is *self-discipline*, comparable to the way self-employment—being your own boss—can act as an analogue of both self-government and self-discipline. In this context, *self-discipline* is just another term for *spiritual freedom*. In this book, *self-discipline* and *spiritual freedom* are synonymous terms; they mean the exact same thing.

In the political context, as a way to unite people on both the left and the right, among other divisions, Voltairine expertly wrote, *"There is one common struggle against those who have appropriated the earth, the money, and the machines."*

I offer Voltairine's unifying approach to the political struggle for peace, equality, and freedom as an analogy of the approach this book takes, not merely to political struggle, but to all struggle and all human suffering.

3

I believe there is one common human struggle in which, whether we like it or not, we find ourselves united, all on the same side, for better or worse.

Superficially, we all struggle with the incessant suffering of common unavoidable discomfort and our human insatiability, the feeling that the grass could always be greener, or is always greener, on the other side. Some would call it, simply, *the human condition*.

If the word "suffering" simply means having unfulfilled desire, then to be human is to suffer. That is because when one fulfills their current desires, more desires emerge. When one reaches their current goals, their mind creates new ones. *"To live is to suffer,"* as Nietzsche put it. You will quicker find a pot of gold at the end of a rainbow than find happiness through achieving goals and fulfilling desires, be they for money, fame, sex, procreation, or whatever. There is always more money to make or more fame to achieve. It is a constant, endless chain of desire. If you get this then you will want that, and if you get that then you will want this, or something else, something more. You cannot eliminate desire by fulfilling desire. Fulfillment causes desire and goals to be replaced, not eliminated. You cannot achieve a state of goallessness by achieving goals. So long as you live as a human, you will have unfulfilled desires and unachieved goals, as the human body and mind will always want more and will invariably create new goals once old goals have been achieved. To be alive is in part to be at war and to struggle.

Humans are united to a degree in our individual struggles through instinctive natural sympathy gifted to us by biological evolution. As two humans, my human suffering entails your suffering because you naturally biologically have a love-like sympathy for me. As natural as it is for your human mouth to water at the smell or sight of delicious food, so too is it natural for your eye to water salty tears from the mental pain of seeing another human in pain. Emphatic mirror neurons fire in your human brain as a reflex, more surely than your foot pops up when a doctor gently hammers your knee.

Thus, even in that merely superficial sense, there is an obvious common human struggle against suffering itself—against pain, discomfort, and any unpleasant human emotion.

The end. Book over.

Just kidding.

The common struggle this book will show goes much deeper. We fight together not merely as evolutionarily programmed robot-like sympathetic social humans desperately seeking to avoid pain, discomfort, and death. Granted, those qualities of our human nature do certainly play a role in our deeper and more spiritual war.

Nonetheless, in addition to our basic reflexive bodily human fight against pain, death, and discomfort, we also fight *for* something, something deeper, something more fundamental, something one can call *spiritual.*

One needn't practice any specific religion or any religion at all to understand it, to recognize it, and to share in it.

A human can win the lottery, become the most famous person in the world, have the grandest beach body you ever did see, and still feel that something is missing.

Still suffer.

Still long for something.

Still not be at peace.

Perhaps our deepest and most known suffering emerges from the lack of achieving that ill-defined thing *for* which we strive, fight, and struggle. Perhaps our deepest suffering may be the suffering felt in the deepest parts of what many would call *your spirit*. Perhaps our greatest and truest pain is not the pain of the body, but the pain of the spirit.

This book seeks to (1) prove that this common uniting struggle *for* something exists, (2) explore and define that thing, and (3) present an effective strategy for working together in peace and in love to obtain this seeming holy grail, to win this war, so to speak—this spiritual war in which all conscious humans find themselves on the same side struggling together.

In calling for equal political freedom, as a contrast to violent classism, Voltairine's wise words of a singular common political struggle ring still to this day to unite people politically across not only the silly one-dimensional left-right political spectrum, but also to unite people politically in a multidimensional way across the whole world and across the ages of time.

When you finish this book, you may in a parallel way find yourself united *spiritually* with every other human being, perhaps even with every other conscious being, human or not, across not only the world but all of the vast seemingly infinite reaches of spacetime.

But first, let's come back down to Earth for a bit.

A World of Problems

In a sense, we live in a world of problems.

In all directions, we see terrible problems, problems that cause suffering and seem to call for desperation and miserable sadness, even anger or full-blown, blood-boiling rage.

We see seemingly preventable problems that we as a species fail to prevent. We see problems to which we both as individuals and as nations contribute. We see problems for which we are the primary cause.

In this world of problems, over ten thousand children starve to death every single day. That is one poor innocent child painfully starving to death every eight seconds or so. At that rate, a handful of innocent children have starved to death since you began reading this chapter, depending on the size of your hand, your hand full of starving children.

Those ten thousand children who starve to death every day ultimately amount to the millions of children who starve to death over the course of a year. They represent a mere fraction of the millions and millions of other innocent children who suffer the excruciating pains of poverty and extreme hunger for years on end until fate maybe finally puts them out of their poor misery with what may be a sadly welcomed death by starvation, all taking place in a world with way more than enough food to feed everyone. For every single innocent child who slowly and painfully starves to death, countless more suffer constantly on the horrible brink of it.

Imagine just one child starving to death, or just one child suffering day after day on the horrendous brink of starvation.

Just one child.

One child suffering and dying.

Picture it.

Now multiply that terrible feeling by millions. These numbers become so massive that we cannot conceptualize them. We could more easily contemplate the seemingly infinite stars and galaxies of the vast universe than bring our conceptual human minds down to Earth to understand the immensity of our own chosen horror. A quote usually attributed to the murderous dictator Stalin goes something like this, *"A single death is a tragedy; a million deaths is a mere statistic."*

Imagine yourself as an alien in a spaceship orbiting Earth watching this horror show, seeing so many innocent children starving to death on one side of this immature planet, while nuclear bombs explode over civilian-filled cities on another side annihilating thousands and thousands of entire families.

Hundreds of thousands of human beings, including countless innocent children, died from the nuclear blasts in Hiroshima and Nagasaki. If you do not call that murder, call it what you want. Stalin would presumably call it a mere statistic. This book seeks not to argue about terminology and semantics.

In a world of abundance, one in which feats of technology and lavish amounts of funding brought humankind to the moon, we allow children to painfully suffer death by starvation—not in isolated incidents of accidental oversight but with the frequent recurring daily regularity of the vicious feeding schedule of a gluttonous murderous vampire. We are vampires who no longer even resist our lifestyle of disregard for human life and human suffering.

While fictional vampires haunt our imaginary nightmares, the unfathomable tragedy of child starvation and other ghoulish symptoms of our own selfishness haunt the incredibly more frightful world to which we wake.

In what ways—really—is a self-serving politician sucking at the profitable teat of the violent military-industrial complex different than a literal vampire murdering children?

Money, riches, ego-stroking fame... are those not all blood by just another name?

Consider, for a moment longer, those countless poor children, who suffer and die from starvation or who violently die from having themselves or their whole family blown to pieces by some intentionally overpriced drone strike. Those poor children epitomize those who suffer most at the cold collective hands of seemingly preventable problems and man-made tragedies.

For those of us who find ourselves on the luckier side of this "tale of two cities", starving children epitomize a much larger *They*. It is the *They* that suffer most.

Focusing on innocent starving children presents a difficulty in the otherwise common knee-jerk reflex of rationalizing, minimizing, or even justifying the seemingly preventable suffering of our fellow human beings.

Do you own a car? How many pairs of shoes do you have? Are you wearing jewelry right now?

Even in consideration of innocent children starving to death, likely at some level you as a human feel that foolish, selfish human instinct: the knee-jerk urge to rationalize or excuse the starvation and death, to somehow conceptually defend the horrible status quo, much like a drug addict creating excuses to use drugs once more, or a blood-addicted vampire creating excuses to murderously pierce another neck and drink.

If you do not feel that knee-jerk urge, then you may be much kinder than the vast majority of humans. Despite that urge to rationalize, minimize, justify, or excuse the suffering of other humans, when the suffering humans are starving children, few would actually say something like the following:

"Starving children deserve it."

"It is their own fault."

"The starving kids need to pull themselves up from their bootstraps."

"I cannot afford to help at all, not more than I already do. There is nothing I could spare, not even a dime more. Even if it would only cost ten cents to save a child's life, I simply could not spare the ten cents."

"Your statistics are wrong. It's not much of a problem."

"Well, what were the starving kids wearing? Maybe they were asking for it."

"There's nothing wrong with children starving, you bleeding-heart snowflake."

Though better repressed when it is young kids dying, there is still even then a natural knee-jerk reactive urge to say such cruel ridiculous things presumably as a way to ease the discomfort of otherwise having to sympathetically acknowledge the suffering of another human being.

However, such actual responses would be more common if, instead of talking about starving children, we spoke of the millions of peaceful human beings suffering in cages like animals in places like the United States. In the United States alone, over two million people currently suffer behind bars—caged and dehumanized, most only accused—not even convicted—of nonviolent crimes, such as marijuana possession. Indeed, many are innocent even of the silly charges acting as the silly rationale for violently forcing another human being into a cage.

"They were asking for it", some would say.

"They deserve it", some would say.

"It's just not my problem", some would say.

Would you embrace the discomfort of truly sympathizing with the millions of peaceful humans suffering in cages? Or would you run from the discomfort?

Detractors may argue the facts of any given case. For instance, the would-be victim I may view as an innocent pacifist prisoner others may view as a nasty criminal responsible for his own miserable imprisonment. What one person genuinely sees as an act of murder another person may see as an unfortunate but necessary use of lethal defensive force.

Some people even deny the Holocaust happened, though this author isn't one of them.

Others may not disagree on the facts of a given case, but rather they have odd moral philosophies. For example, some people excuse or even support non-defensive violence such as murder, rape, and slavery as long as it is done by the government or the police—as long as it is legal. In other words, they hold man-made laws in higher esteem than they hold any criminals like the repeatedly arrested criminal Dr.

Martin Luther King Jr., or the not only arrested but executed criminal legends like Jesus and Socrates, two of the most famous legendary executed criminals, considered shameless breakers of man-made law.

Remember, earlier in this book it was written that one of the most dangerous and controversial topics on which to speak—or act—is love and peace, because even just in speaking support for love one thereby challenges haters, and by speaking in support of peace one challenges the violent. By standing in front of those who would throw stones, one stands in front of stones. Jesus said to love your enemies, so naturally the government murdered him.

Consider someone whose compass is guided by reverence for the classist authority of man-made laws, referring to the self-proclaimed authority of one group of humans using non-defensive violence to boss around another group of people. A group of people is just a class in political lingo. Thus, all non-defensive violence is simply a form of classism. The violent aggressor—meaning the person or group using non-defensive violence—is ipso facto engaging in classism, to make themselves ruler and another the ruled, to make themselves the violent dominator and the other the dominated.

One who endorses such violence simply because it is legal is one who would support rape, such as prima nocta. Presumably, that kind of person watches the fictionalized movie *Braveheart* and roots against William Wallace and roots for the law-abiding rapists. Presumably, that kind of person watches *Star Wars*, and is on the side of the Empire. Presumably, that kind of person cheers when the Death Star laser nukes an entire planet that might as well be called Planet Hiroshima or Planet Nagasaki.

When we talk about adults starving to death instead of merely children, or soldiers killing adults rather than killing innocent children, detractors would more quickly give in to the knee-jerk reaction of wanting to believe the suffering was somehow deserved, somehow caused by the alleged victim, or somehow not a call to invest oneself heavily in unselfish reform of the status quo.

Generally speaking, whether we give into it or not, we can all relate to that natural knee-jerk urge to avoid the discomfort of simple honest sympathy for a suffering human.

As an individual human, I have my personal opinions including opinions regarding the millions of nonviolent human beings suffering in cages throughout the United States, themselves the victims of non-defensive violence committed by a blatantly plutocratic oligarchy parading around as a democracy, not that two wolves eating a sheep would make the violence more tolerable. Between campaign contributions, kickbacks, and paid lobbyists, alleged democracy is but a shell game.

This book is not about my individual human opinions or beliefs, and you do not need to share my empirical beliefs on any political or material matters for us to agree on the deep spiritual truths this book seeks to help reveal. We need not agree on any matter of politics or religion to both see the beautiful common struggle uniting every single one of us. Indeed, there likely isn't a single human being on this planet who agrees with another human being on everything, but yet there is so much upon which we can easily agree.

This book seeks to present deep spiritual truths that are very agreeable to all, most of which are self-evident truths.

You do not need to be of a certain religion to read this book, nor will you need to change your religion to accept the truths presented in this book. This book is written for readers of all religions, including the non-religious. Without changing their religion, readers of all religions, including non-religion, can realize their place in the common struggle that unites us.

This book seeks to unite diverse readers of all sorts, of all cultures, religions, and belief systems, without infringing on anyone's spiritual freedom.

Perhaps the most crucial aspect of the wonderful beauty of freedom *is* the creative diversity that the freedom engenders.

This book is written for readers from all sides of the absurdly oversimplified one-dimensional left-right political spectrum, and so too is this book for those who refuse to place themselves on that abruptly oversimplified one-dimensional spectrum at all. In other words, you do not need to be politically liberal or politically conservative to read this book, but you can be. Regardless, you will not need to become more or less right-wing or left-wing in your political beliefs to accept the truths in this book.

You do not need to be pro-vaccine, anti-vaccine, or something in between to read this book, to agree with its truths, and to unite with your fellow human beings in our shared beautiful common struggle. To agree with the truths in this book and realize your unity with every other human being, you do not and will not need to change your attitude about vaccines as a whole if you even have such an attitude about vaccines as a whole. You will not need to change your opinion about any one specific vaccine, assuming you have a more nuanced way of dealing with that matter that does not treat all vaccines exactly the same. And if you have no opinions on vaccines at all, you can continue having no such opinion.

If you cheer against William Wallace when watching *Braveheart* and cheer against the criminal Jedi rebels when watching *Star Wars*, I

14

will never agree with you on that, and may choose to avoid watching movies with you, but for the purposes of the truths this book presents and regarding the common struggle that unites us as conscious human beings, that's totally okay.

In fact, Darth Vader is actually kind of cool; I do admit.

A significant aspect of what allows the truths in this book to transcend the typical divisions that divide us is that this book doesn't claim that we *should* become united, whatever that would mean. Rather, this book seeks to have the reader realize we already *are* united, whether we like it or not.

Truth is something that can be revealed, not something that can be done. There are no *shoulds* or *oughts* when it comes to truth. Truth is simply a matter of what *is*.

In addition to showing the unity between you and me and starving children, this book will show the unity between you, me, and those who have a different religion than us.

This book will show the unity between you, me, and those who have different partisan politics than us.

This book will show the unity between you, me, and those who prefer to order a different flavor doughnut from the doughnut shop, or a different style of coffee.

This book will show the unity between you, me, and everyone.

Our eyes may see different things, but some agreeable uniting truths can be seen even with your eyes closed, and we all see those.

As fallible humans, there is a metaphorical sense in which our eyes are always closed. There is a sense in which the kinds of unifying spiritual truths I have promised to show with this book are the kinds of truths you can trust most faithfully and with the most certainty. In other words, you can typically be most certain of what you see with your eyes closed, for even your own eyes can deceive you.

Anything you see with your literal eyes is doubtable, but some truths are beyond even a shadow of a doubt.

Those undoubtable truths are the kinds of truth you can see even with your eyes closed.

This book does not claim to hold each and every one of those eyes-closed truths that exist, only some of them. This book doesn't claim to hold the whole truth, the whole agreeable eyes-closed truth, but rather some of it.

To claim this book holds all such truths would be to deny each reader their unique religion, their unique politics, their unique opinions. It would be to reject the beautiful diversity engendered by freedom of spirit. To be redundant, much of the beauty of freedom is in the diversity it engenders, and, for that reason, this book in no way seeks to minimize that beautiful diversity.

Though they have their many differences, one can also find some wonderful fundamental threads of shared truth weaving through all of the major religions in the world, common-ground truths about unconditional love, forgiveness, and this dream-like life itself. We can see these truths even in the ancient myths and extinct religions that nobody holds as true now, including but not limited to the ancient Greek stories of tempting sirens, of Sisyphus's boulder, of Icarus burning off his wings by flying too close to the sun.

This book seeks to warm, without burning.

This book seeks to illuminate, without blinding.

This book seeks to free, without infringing.

This book seeks to save, without imposing.

I ask for nothing but some time and an open mind, with the hope to leave us united and inspired, with   diverse togetherness, with the open-ended creativity that beautifully emerges from spiritual freedom.

Why We Don't Help Them,
They That Seem to Suffer Most

One might ask, why don't we help them, they who suffer most?

One might ask, in this world of seemingly preventable problems, why do we not prevent the preventable problems? Why do we not solve the solvable problems?

More specifically, for instance, one might ask, why don't we feed the thousands and thousands of children who starve to death every day?

Why do so many of us spend more money on expensive cars and perfume than we donate to charity? How come we find the time, money, and energy to buy and drink alcohol, buy and smoke cigarettes, and buy and drink soda, but we cannot help starving kids?

Whether it is starvation, malaria, or something else, it doesn't cost much financially to save a young human life.

In the first world, such as in the USA, it would not be out of the ordinary to stumble upon a morbidly obese cigarette-smoking alcoholic Republican passionately debating a morbidly obese cigarette-smoking alcoholic Democrat about why healthcare costs so much, or why healthcare costs are rising, before both speed off, exceeding an already high speed limit in overpriced homicidal death machines that cost them each a thousand dollars a month every month in stressful high-interest bills, month after month.

What more evidence would one need that the Cosmos makes jokes?

The question is why: Why do we seem to behave so selfishly? Why don't we do more to help?

One answer that would be sufficient if it was true would be that we are psychopaths. If we had no empathy, then that closes the case. No need to call Sherlock.

But we are not psychopaths.

We have empathy.

We have an innate form of love-like sympathy for our fellow human beings.

For the sake of argument, we can temporarily ignore consciousness and spirituality, meaning we can conceptually play around with pretend absurd zombie-physicalism, imagining people as all being *philosophical zombies*, meaning hypothetical people who outwardly seem conscious but aren't really. Even then, there is still an unconscious love-like nature to our basic natural evolved machinery that emerges from our so-called selfish genes, selfish genes which result in emergent innate empathy, sympathy, and altruistic-style behavior at the macroscopic scale of everyday life, such as a mother sacrificing her own life to save her baby, or a warrior ant sacrificing its life for its colony, or a soldier jumping on a grenade to save his companions. Even in a world of spirit-less philosophical zombies lacking true consciousness, still even then, from selfish simplicity, emerges intelligent altruistic-like complexity.

Point being, we would have to be abnormal psychopaths to not sympathize at some level to some degree with other humans in pain.

But we aren't psychopaths.

Granted, there are some literal human psychopaths on this planet, but they would have already put this book down by this point, so I have good evidence for thinking uniquely well of you. Even without that, I'll give you the benefit of the doubt on this if you give it to me: You and I are not psychopaths.

Based on countless factors and circumstances in any given situation, we do vary the degree to which we express, act on, or suppress our natural sympathy towards other humans, but the sympathy instinct is still there even if suppressed, reduced, or not acted upon due to extenuating circumstances. For example, our outwardly displayed sympathy may be greater for someone whose house is burned down by a freak accident through no fault of their own versus an angry arsonist who angrily burns down their own house in a fit of foolish rage. We may sympathize more with the murder victim than the suicidal person. A racist may—as ridiculous as it seems to the rest of us—display more sympathy towards someone who has a skin tone closer to their own.

Regardless, ultimately, with the exception of rare literal psychopaths, we do sympathize.

Thus, the reason for our failure to help the extremely less fortunate is neither psychopathy nor simple selfishness.

As the next chapter will show, quite the opposite is the case actually: We can't help starving children because we can't even help ourselves.

We Can't Help Starving Children
Because We Can't Help Ourselves

To be fair, it's not clear the degree to which it is can't versus don't, but either way, the result is the same: We don't even help ourselves.

Thus, to an extent, it is fair to conclude, for most intents and purposes, we cannot help ourselves since one would think if we could, we would.

It's not extreme selfishness, let alone full-blown psychopathy, that is the cause of our failure to save starving children among needy others, but rather the opposite: it is our self-destructiveness.

We may behave cruelly and behave in seemingly unsympathetic ways toward starving children and others who suffer, but it isn't because we selfishly treat them worse than we treat ourselves. The sad opposite is the case: We treat them so cruelly because we treat them like we treat ourselves, which is cruelly.

Many children these days are taught something, often called The Golden Rule: *Treat others how you want to be treated.*

If we judge the way someone wants to be treated by how they treat themselves, then the seeming problems in this seeming world of problems can be explained simply by an unfortunate following of The Golden Rule.

We treat ourselves badly. We are cruel to ourselves. We habitually behave unsympathetically and unlovingly to the very human we see in the mirror.

In the USA, official suicide is both one of the leading causes of death for teenagers and for the elderly.

And that refers only to situations in which suicide is officially listed as the cause of death on documentation. Documented suicide does not include an alcoholic who dies in a crash while drunk driving. Documented suicide doesn't include most lethal drug overdoses. Documented suicide does not include a life-long cigarette-smoker who dies of lung cancer. If we documented it more accurately, perhaps we'd all be documented as suicidal self-harmers.

Even for those of us who find ourselves on the wildly luckier and wildly more luxurious side in this unfair "tale of two cities", we still suffer so very deeply—*at our own hands, at our own doing.*

Simple psychopathic selfishness is not what drives an alcoholic to drink himself to death.

Simple psychopathic selfishness is not what causes someone with an extreme case of low self-esteem to wake up, look in the mirror and think, if not say aloud to that human in the mirror, *"I hate you,"* or *"You're ugly and disgusting."*

Simple psychopathic selfishness is not what causes a wealthy neglected trust-fund baby to cut her wrists vertically, bleeding out to death by her own hand, crying.

Simple psychopathic selfishness is not what causes a morbidly obese person to overeat to death, which quite literally happens many times every day. Obesity is currently one of the leading causes of human death. According to the World Health Organization, nearly three million people die every year from obesity.[1] That's over 8,000

---

[1] https://www.who.int/news-room/facts-in-pictures/detail/6-facts-on-obesity

human beings per day, killed literally by their own hands shoveling excessive food down their own throat.

If thousands of innocent children starving to death every day is considered a preventable problem, what irony it is that in this "tale of two cities" it is such a similarly common problem for food addicts and sugar addicts to overeat to death.

If it isn't food, maybe it's a heroin needle or one too many glasses full of whiskey, presumably consumed by a sad person, a person not only driven to addiction by sadness but also driven to sadness by addiction, yet unwilling to sacrifice the comfort of that addiction as self-medication for the very misery it exacerbates.

Addictive objects and behaviors, such as crack cocaine (the object) or the act of smoking it (the behavior), are sometimes called "vices", "sins", "bad habits", or "temptations". They can sometimes be referred to with words like "short-sighted", "indulgent", "evil", or "unhealthy". The words vary by specific substance, specific behavior, and by the preferences and vernacular of the speaker. Some people prefer some words; some prefer others. A given religious person talking about a certain thing might favor the word "sin", while a therapist talking to their own client might prefer the phrase, "undesirable habit you are struggling to change". As stated earlier, this book seeks not to argue terminology or semantics. Call these things what you want, and vary what you call them as you see fit. Whatever you usually call them, we can agree that they are ***props in the common human struggle against temptation and misery***.

I call them many things, but one thing I like to call them is *props*. In this crazy little play on this crazy little stage called Earth, *props* seems like an appropriate name.

Consider our greed, our overindulgence, our money-addicted materialism, and our gluttony. These are various symptoms and varying words for a shared fundamental quality; call it what you will. Whatever you call it, it is by itself as problematic as the problems it seems to cause. That underlying, seemingly problematic thing is our self-cruelty and our apparent lack of self-love. Excessive selfishness such as greedy gluttony merely exemplifies a deeper pattern of self-destructiveness, temptation-caving, and seeming self-hatred, which exist not just between us as individuals in a species but also—and even more so—*within* each of us as individuals.

The battle is mostly, if not entirely, inside.

For those of us who haven't yet killed ourselves with any of the various tempting props and siren songs including but not limited to those mentioned, we nonetheless use the props to inflict terrible damage and great suffering upon the human we see in the mirror, be it from overeating or anorexia, alcohol or cigarettes, laziness or gym-rat egomania, shopaholic-induced credit card debt or gambling addiction, this or that, vice or sin, yours or mine.

The enemy is within.

I previously quoted the tyrant Stalin, so it is only fair I quote one of the prisoners who suffered in a soviet gulag under Stalin's rule, a nonviolent criminal who, unlike many of the nonviolent human beings suffering in prison today, was actually guilty of the crime for which he was charged: criticizing Stalin. To that end, I quote a passage from *The Gulag Archipelago* by Aleksandr Solzhenitsyn:

> *If only it were all so simple! If only there were evil people somewhere insidiously committing evil deeds, and it were necessary only to separate them from the rest of us and destroy them. But the line dividing good and evil cuts through the heart of every human being.*

Why We Can't Help Ourselves: The Two Yous

The previous chapter ends with a wise quote from a convicted criminal who proposed that the line between so-called "good" and so-called "evil" cuts through the heart of every human being. Even if we drop the unnecessary moralizing language, we can still see that we are each in many ways cut into two.

When we speak about '*you*', there are actually at least two different *yous* about whom we speak.

That is not a reference to some kind of philosophical metaphysical dualism. Rather, the truths in this book are agreeable to metaphysical dualists and monists alike. One could even argue that the differences between most forms of dualism and monism are merely semantics. In fact, some philosophers argue that all philosophy is just word games. Regardless, those are not arguments for this book.

Rather, this duality is a conceptual duality, not a metaphysical duality.

In analogy, if one claims that the vague term '*your computer*' can refer to two different things: *your laptop* or *your desktop*, it doesn't propose some grand philosophical dualism entailing a magical realm of laptop-substance versus desktop-substance. Rather, the conceptual duality and two meanings for the same word are simply a symptom of the vagueness and equivocality of human language.

It's not controversial to say there are two *Yous*, meaning two distinct things going by the label *You*, just as it is not controversial to say there may be two things going by the label *your computer*.

So what are the two *Yous*?

The first *You*, we can call *The Real You* or *Your Consciousness*. Some would call it your spirit, your true self, your spiritual self, your higher self, your inner heavenly parent, your essence, the dreamer, or your soul.

The second *You*, we can call *your false self, your ego*, or *your body*. Some would call it your lower self, your bodily self, your body itself, your avatar, your vessel, your ship, your form, your inner demon, your lizard brain, the beast inside the man, or the primitive self.

Those different terms are just labels, mere semantics.

If what this book calls *the real you* is something you prefer to call *your soul* or *your spirit*, that's fine. If you prefer to call it *your consciousness* or *higher self*, that's fine too. This book uses all those phrases interchangeably. Feel free to pick your preferred phrase and swap it in anytime the others are used if you prefer to reserve certain terms for some other idea outside of the scope of this unifying book and the highly agreeable but limited truths this book explores.

The same goes for what this book usually calls *the false self* or *ego*. Feel free to swap out the terms. If you prefer, call it the primitive self, the lower self, the egoic self, the non-spiritual self, the body, your ever-changing form, the changing form of your unifying essence, the would-be philosophical zombie you illuminate with your undeniable consciousness, or the sinful flesh inhabited by your heavenly soul.

Call it whatever you want because—to paraphrase the wisdom of Shakespeare's Juliet—*a rose by any other name smells just as sweet.*

We must not cling to terms if we want to peacefully and productively speak and listen in ways that both (1) welcome the beautiful diversity that freedom engenders and (2) are understood by people who don't happen to share our specific religious or philosophical views. In other words, we must be very flexible with our labels, and we must be charitable with our interpretations of others' words. That is, assuming we want to do more than preach to our respective choirs.

Regardless of what words this book uses, this book neither proposes nor denies any religious or metaphysical claims, such as dualism. Even when this book uses the word "soul" or "spirit", it is used in a way that is compatible with atheism and scientific materialism, as well as compatible with dualism or the ontology of any major religion. In this context, *spirit* simply means *consciousness*. And in the words of the infamous atheist and neuroscientist Sam Harris: *"Consciousness is the one thing in this universe that cannot be an illusion."*

Even the most devout believer in skeptical scientific atheistic materialism can agree that these two different Yous exist just as they can agree two different computers exist, a given laptop and a given desktop, or that two different components of a singular computer exist such as a monitor versus a motherboard. Philosophers can argue about whether there is a meaningful distinction between a dualistic interpretation versus a monistic interpretation of these separate components, and, if so, which interpretation more accurately describes reality. Such philosophers can debate what explains the so-called correlates of consciousness, of specific conscious experiences, in the material human brain. That is all far beyond the scope of this unifying book.

The duality and equivocalness of our language is something upon which even an adamant atheist and a devout religious person can easily agree, as well as anyone else.

In the narrow context of this book, the duality of what we call You is simply a facet of equivocal language, where we use the one word to refer to two things: (1) *the real you*, meaning *your consciousness*, versus (2) the rest of your unconscious mind and body.

You have a human body,
but you are not human.

René Descartes famously provided the proof that the real you, your consciousness, exists.

"Cogito ergo sum."

"I think, therefore I am."

Descartes wisely pointed out that even if all your experiences are illusions and all your empirical beliefs are false, they still prove the existence of *you*, the conscious experiencer of those potentially false experiences. Even a hallucination requires a hallucinator.

Philosophically speaking, the physical human you see in the mirror may not really exist.

Philosophically speaking, humans may not really exist at all, but rather may be an imagined type of creature, of the same type as unicorns or Santa Claus. Philosophically speaking, you could be a non-human alien dreaming right now, and when you awaken you may tell your alien friends about this wild dream you had about these fictional creatures called humans—and that you dreamed you were one, a human, and forgot you were dreaming. Perhaps your alien friends will giggle as you tell them tales of our goofy pretend human antics.

Humans may not exist, but you—*the real you*—definitely exist.

In that sense, you—*the real you*—are definitely not human because you possess something humans don't: definitive undeniable existence.

Do not take the following use of the word "spirit" to assert (or deny) anything religious, magical, or supernatural. I simply use the word here to refer to the same thing as I have referred to above with the words *the real you* and *your consciousness*.

With that said, there is a wise saying that goes like this: "*You do not have a spirit. You are a spirit. You have a body.*"

At least, that is, if your human eyes and the mirror are to be believed, then you have a body, a human body. However, philosophically speaking, there is inherently something circular to the logic of trusting your human eyes to spot a human in the mirror. The philosophical basis for having any faith in science, empirical matters, and perception at all is logically circular and, in that way, not beyond doubt.

In any case, with absolute agreeable certainty, we can say that you, *the real you*, are not human; you are the undeniable consciousness that empirically (i.e. deniably) seems to be correlated with the deniable human. In other words, you seem to have a human body at the moment, the keyword being 'seem'.

We can now see the value of having clarified earlier that the word "You" refers to two different things. Otherwise, the agreeable fact that you are not human might seem jarring. But of course it is only one of the two Yous that is not human. The "You" we have called "the real you", which some would call "your soul" or "your spirit", is not human and is clearly not even tangible. The other "you", the unreal you, the body, is human—if it even exists.

That may raise the question, to what extent is this human body of yours a vessel you steer versus a prison.

Even if it turns out that neither Earth nor humans really exist at all except as fictional artifacts in some alien dream or AI-built Matrix, that question is still actually meaningful.

That is because even a dream can become an out-of-control nightmare, especially insofar as you forget your true power, namely your power of choice, or mistake yourself as a passive observer rather than a free-spirited creative transcendental entity.

Even a god can accidentally create a hell with a population of one: himself.

But these questions of inner peace and nightmares, and the godliness of creative dreamers, are questions for later.

Let's first, in a bit more depth, explore this matter of you definitely not being human.

Your Clothes,
Figurative or Otherwise

With a buffet of deliciously diverse terminology, the previous chapter showed that you—the real you—are not human. You have a human body, which you wear like clothes and inhabit like a car, but you—the real you—are the consciousness, not its ever-changing outfit or vehicle. The figurative clothing that is your body is one day vibrantly young then later worn and wrinkly. But yet there is a more static consciousness—you—that is shared between those different outfits, the young body and the aged body.

The human creature may or may not really exist, but the real you, conscious and inhuman as you are, definitely does exist in the most absolutely real sense. You not only remain if you wake up in a slightly older body, but so too if you wake up as a non-human alien having had a crazy dream, or as the opening question asked, woke up in my body as the human I see in the mirror.

With that reiterated, let's put aside the extreme philosophical skepticism and speak with a little more everyday practicality, where we treat questions of existence or reality as relative to this empirically observed world, without regard to the possibility that it may be a dream or Matrix, with its made-up constructs of Newtonian-like time and space, with its imaginarily solid objects, from the big to the point-like, in which we faithfully can say humans do seem to exist and unicorns do not, at least according to current empirical evidence.

In this relative world of constructs, what are you, really?

What defines *the real you*?

That which defines a thing, meaning that which is true about it by definition, cannot change over the lifespan of that thing. If a bachelor gets married, he is no longer a bachelor because being unmarried is a defining characteristic of bachelorhood. If a planet evaporates and no longer has mass, it is no longer a planet—assuming having mass is a defining characteristic of being a planet. Thus, these can be called *defining traits*.

What doesn't define a thing can change over the course of that thing's existence, or lifespan, without the thing itself being considered destroyed. A bachelor can get a haircut and still be a bachelor. A planet's climate can become colder, starting an ice age, and it is still a planet. The tree in my backyard can grow bigger or smaller, and it would still be "the tree in my backyard". These traits are called *non-defining traits*. These are things that may happen to be true about a thing at a certain time, but don't ever define it, and thus can change and are never *necessarily* true about it.

The bachelor may have hair, and that hair may have color, but those are not defining traits of bachelorhood. Being unmarried is a defining trait of bachelorhood.

Another set of terminology some philosophers use to discuss this idea of defining traits versus changeable non-defining traits is to speak of what may or may not be *synthetically* or *accidentally* true about something versus what is *analytically* or *necessarily* true about it (i.e. true by definition). In this sense, synthetic truths ("The bachelor over there is engaged to Mary") may or may not be true, and the truth of such a *synthetic* statement can change over time, depending on how

36

the relationship between the *synthesized* components changes. In the given example, the *synthesized* components are primarily (1) the bachelor, (2) Mary, and (3) a time. In contrast, *analytic* truths are true by definition (e.g. "The bachelor is unmarried," "two plus two equals four") and are thus true eternally.

A defining trait is necessarily always true about something by definition, not just always within time but also in the deeper sense of timelessness, meaning also *outside of time* such as in some Platonic-like eternal world of forms, not to suggest such a place literally exists.

So what defines you, *the real you*? In other words, what qualities must some *thing* have for that *thing* to be you?

What limited set of traits about the current synthetic creature reading this book is *the real you*? Which are merely changeable traits of the ever-changing meatsuit you wear like figurative clothing? What can be taken away or destroyed without destroying you, the real you? What could be destroyed or cease to exist, but *you* would still exist?

For instance, your socks or wristwatch don't define you, the real you, because you could take those off, throw them in a fire, and you would still exist and be you, the real you.

Assuming you existed a year ago and still exist today, what unchanging constants existed then and remain now that define you? What would need to exist ten years from now for you to say that you—the real you—still exist at that time? Your hair? No. Your pinky finger? No. Those could be destroyed or replaced, and you would still remain.

Process of elimination can be helpful. So let's run through a nice long pretty list of all the things you are not.

You are not your literal clothes.

You may look in the mirror one day and see a blue shirt and look in the mirror the next day and see a red shirt.

You can take your shirt off right now and burn it. Destroying your shirt does not destroy you, the real you. The shirt would be gone but you, *the real you,* would still be there.

Your literal clothes, or your wardrobe as a whole, may be a big or a small part of your changeable egoic self, which we can alternatively call *your false self.*

Indeed, for some humans, their literal outfits represent a huge part of their ego.

Insofar as the outfit is easily stripped, it can represent an especially sensitive part of a sensitive ego.

For example, consider when Gordon Ramsay dramatically yells, "*Take off your jacket,*" in his reality show Hell's Kitchen.

In another example, consider a new police officer who, after working hard to earn his job, understandably walks around wearing his badge and uniform with so much egoic pride, but one day he finds through misfortune that he may lose his job—and his uniform—unless he lies under oath or commits some other deceitful and harmful act that under more normal circumstances he would not commit. To lose his badge and uniform may feel like losing himself, at least that is to the degree he falsely identifies with or possessively clings to that egoic role of uniformed police officer, a temporary pseudo-identity.

In yet another example, presumably outfits and uniforms played a significant role in the infamous Stanford Prison Experiment.

Both threatened egos and stroked egos can be very dangerous, indeed.

Clothes, outfits, and entire wardrobes can be a significant characteristic of an ego, of a false self, or of a full-blown pseudo-identity.

But such clothes aren't a defining trait of you, the real you. You can change your clothes, even let go of your entire wardrobe, let go emotionally, or literally give away the whole shebang to other humans, and still you would be you, *the real you.*

Therefore, your clothes are not you, not even really a part of the real you, and not a true defining characteristic of you.

You are not your figurative clothes either.

Just as you, *the real you*, are not your literal clothes, you are also not your figurative clothes, which include the following:

You are not your name.
You are not your money.
You are not your degrees or certificates.
You are not your job.
You are not your social security number.
You are not your eye color, eye size, or eye shape.
You are not your hair color, hair style, or hair volume.
You are not your gender.
You are not your skin tone or skin color.
You are not your credit score.
You are not your ego, whether it's big, small, proud, or ashamed.
You are not your ego's egotistical thoughts, feelings, or urges.
You are not your reputation or what other people think of you.
You are not the specific collection of atoms and molecules in your body.
You are not your memories.
You are not really your body at all.

You are none of those changeable things, nor anything like them. You are not defined by any of these things, meaning none of them are defining characteristics of you. They can change, and you would still be you, the real you.

Even though none of the things listed in the above list are defining characteristics of *the real you*, they may be a defining characteristic of a character you play sometimes, acting as a temporary pseudo-identity, an egoic form or a false self, like a role played by an actor. And a good actor seemingly becomes the role, sometimes purposefully forgetting their true self.

If at a given time you happen to have a certain job, it may require wearing a uniform, it may require having certain educational credentials, or it may come with a verifiable badge number, any of which if taken away may cause that pseudo-identity to be destroyed or die. In that way, they are defining characteristics of that role at that time, but you are not the role, and its defining characteristics are not yours.

Consider the meaning behind phrases like *"New year, new me,"* which presumably usually mean something like, *"My old false self from last year is dead, and this new different false self is reborn in its place."*

It is analogous to taking off one pair of shoes and putting on another: *New year, new shoes*. You never are your shoes. You never are your changeable clothes, figurative or otherwise.

In this sense, your entire personality is like an outfit of clothing, except the plural—*personalities*—probably fits better in case you have several: maybe one for your friends, one for your family, and a third for that attractive cashier at your favorite store.

Like an actor starring in multiple TV shows at once, a person can have many false sub-identities at once, different roles they play in different contexts. All figurative clothing.

You can temporarily take on new roles and lose old ones. The roles do not define you.

Like a retired actor, you will still be you, the real you, even if you give up all of your current roles.

These roles are themselves individualized instances or pieces of the second of *the two yous,* meaning *the false self.* In many ways, the false self is thus a collection of changing roles, pseudo-identities, and their various ever-changing material characteristics (e.g. eye color, weight, height, badge number, personality, etc.), all of which you wear like clothing sometimes. Today the unreal you could be red-shirt-guy and tomorrow the unreal you could be blue-shirt-guy. The real you is not ever defined by its shirt or shirt color, or by whether or not it's a guy at all.

Likewise, the real you is not defined by hair color, eye color, gender, size, weight, job, age, bank account, financial net worth, degrees, certificates, wardrobes, uniforms, atomic molecules, or memories. The real you is not defined by titles like doctor, nurse, or doctorate. The real you is not defined by how much you can bench press or how fast you can run a mile. The real you is not even defined by how many legs you have. We could amputate both legs on that human meatsuit you see in the mirror, and you would still be you, *the real you.* The double amputation might affect the time it takes for that human meatsuit you call a body to run a mile, but blessings usually come in disguise.

It's odd to follow such a weird out-of-place joke with some of the wisest words I've ever read, but I'm an odd fellow. On the subject of actual blessings in disguise, here is a truly enlightened Sufi proverb:

"When the ego weeps for what it has lost, the spirit rejoices for what it has found."

To illustrate in modern terms the wisdom of that proverb, let this be said: It can be liberating to realize you are not your credit score if your credit score is embarrassingly low. It can be liberating to realize you are not the car you drive, and you are not defined by the car you drive, if you drive a piece of cheap junk or are too broke to even have a car. It can be liberating to realize you are not your body or would-be good looks if it looks as though you fell off the ugly tree and hit every branch on the way down. But now consider the opposite. Consider you haven't yet been blessed with such discomfort and misfortune. If you proudly drive the most expensive car ever made, without a scratch on it, your ego may scream in denial as you read my words saying you aren't your car and that the car doesn't define the real you. If you have a doctorate from an Ivy League school and couldn't be prouder when you put on your status-symbolizing lab coat or your expensive work suit, your prideful ego might scream in denial as I say the real you is not defined by your job, degrees, certificates, clothes, or uniform.

Your ego, or false self, can scream in denial at my words above.

But it's not just me that egos and false selves will need to deny; it is the self-evident truth which time will prove again and again to each who doubts it. The truth does not need me or anyone to speak it. The thing about changeable things like clothes, careers, and cars is that they change eventually no matter what. No matter how possessively or egotistically one clings to such things, the sands of time will take them away in less than the blink of a cosmic eye.

The job will one day end. The car will one day be sold for parts. The most attractive fashion model in the world will age, wrinkle, and scar. Even the happiest marriage in the world will end eventually, by death or divorce.

It's those human beings with the prettiest faces and the most expensive cars, the most esteemed jobs, and the most glamorous wardrobes, who will tend to find the above words hardest to hear. The comfort zone is a sticky dark trap, a spiritual prison for those who aren't careful.

Even if they choose not to heed the words above, those who have not been blessed by discomfort yet will be soon. Life has a beautiful way of knocking over all pedestals in short time, but be it short or long, eventually, time destroys all clothes, both figurative and literal, and thus the beautiful nakedness beneath is always revealed.

Humpty Dumpty:
Let's Put You Back Together Again

In the previous chapter, we conceptually stripped you of your figurative clothes.

Through the process of elimination, we aimed to find what defines *the real you* by first stripping away the many coverings that do not define the real you.

We stripped away your ego and your changing roles: you are not your ego or your job. You are not defined by your job or professional title.

We stripped away your money, your meaty muscles, and your facial appearances: You are not your face, muscles, or finances. You are not defined by your credit score or how much money you have in the bank. You are not defined by how much weight you lift in the gym, nor by how many jaws drop when you walk through the mall in tight pants, whether from attraction or horror.

We stripped away your hair if you aren't bald already, your school degrees if you even graduated, and your car if you are lucky enough to even have one.

We stripped away your memories, your eye color, your skin color, and even your name.

All this stripping away of fabric, all this stripping thread by thread at the very fabric that one might otherwise mistake as the real you, may leave you feeling a bit shattered or broken apart.

Indeed, we stand now in a pool of shredded tossed away figurative fabric, the shattered remains of the unreal you.

Let's put you back together again.

The trick to putting Humpty Dumpty back together is to realize that he never was his shell. The shell was a mask all along.

By knocking him down and shattering his shell into pieces, we haven't destroyed him; we have provided him the means of his spiritual liberation.

Humpty Dumpty doesn't need a surgeon. He simply needs to find himself. He simply needs to find *his true self* in the carnage of his shattered shell, perhaps for the first time ever.

We don't need to call an ambulance for Humpty. We need to call a Buddhist monk, a Taoist sage, a Jewish rabbi, or a Christian priest. Any spiritual teacher will do, and even for those who find themselves physically alone, through choice or otherwise, time can teach all.

Time is a spiritual teacher, brutal but effective. There are no gatekeepers for eyes-closed truths.

If Humpty Dumpty is not conscious, meaning if Humpty Dumpty is a *philosophical zombie,* then he does not have a true self, neither in the sense of *the real you,* nor in the sense in which Descartes wrote *Cogito Ergo Sum.*

Despite the typical translation, for Descartes's argument to work, it is actually not enough for one to merely think and have thought. One cannot truly understand and use Descartes's argument if one only has merely *unconscious* thoughts. Rather, what makes Descartes's argument so incredibly profound and meaningful is the reference to conscious awareness, namely conscious awareness of thought, the *conscious hearing* of the inner monologue generated by most human brains.

You are not that which thinks the thoughts, but rather that which consciously hears or observes the thoughts.

Humpty Dumpty may be a philosophical zombie, meaning he may be merely full of air. If that's the case, then he's out of luck.

But you aren't full of air.

You are conscious.

Wait, there it is.

After all of that "you are not this" and "you are not that", finally it is written, a sentence about what you are: "You are conscious."

If not, then you are not. That's the other side of Descartes's argument, and it's quite literally the case. If you are a *philosophical zombie*, then there is no *real you*, at least not in the way described in this book. If you are a philosophical zombie, then there is only the one you, not the two yous.

Even a philosophical zombie would tend to have all of the things we stripped away: hair, shoes, a car, a brain, eyes, money, a degree, a job. That's all part of the changing shell, the changing clothing.

If you are not truly conscious, then there is only your Humpty-Dumpty-like shell, and after breaking that shell into pieces, after shredding and stripping all that away, there would be nothing left, no real you underneath.

Luckily, since I'm not a solipsist, I have faith that that is not the case. I have faith that you are not full of air. In other words, I believe you are conscious just like I am and just like Descartes was. In yet other words, I believe *the real you* does exist. I believe when we break the shell and strip the clothes, you are there, existing. Consciousness exists. *You* exist.

There: You just found yourself, your true self. What a wonderful spiritual feat!

Book over. The end. Just kidding. Again.

Jokes aside, even though you may have "found yourself"—meaning your true self, *the real you*—before reading this book, whether in the Humpty-Dumpty way described above or in a different way, that is no trivial accomplishment. Many humans seem to go through this life without ever finding themselves in that way. Some humans will say over and over for years that they are "trying to find themselves", but they often seem to do it by chasing money, fame, drugs, alcohol, sex partners, fancy cars, jewelry, good looks, fashion, food, passport stamps, and so on and so forth. Some say they want to find themselves but all they seem to do is look for new pieces of shell to add to their Humpty-Dumpty outer layer, placing new walls and more padding on their prison if anything. A new degree. A new car. A new spouse. A new tattoo. Another pizza. As if enlightenment or the real you was found at the bottom of a whiskey glass or as part of a promotion at your day job.

In any case, you likely had already done it in your own way before reading this book, but, if not, then we did it now. We found you, the real you. You genuinely deserve to take a moment and appreciate that accomplishment. You did something that many never will.

And these are not just poetic words or platitudes. It's truly worth something to have found yourself, your true self, in this way. It truly gives you something special you can hold onto, reliably.

You can, and inevitably will, lose your fancy car, your good looks, your fame, your awesome career, and any other material things. In contrast, that which you found when you found yourself, the real you, will always be there for you. Again, this is not mere poetry or platitudes. It goes right back to the idea of unchanging defining traits—eternal timeless truths—versus changeable non-defining traits (i.e. figurative clothing). By definition, as long as you are, you are. You eternally have you, the real you. In the same absolute necessary eternal *a priori* sense that we can say that two plus two equals four, you will always have you no matter what body you find yourself in, what planet you find yourself on, what year it is, or what you see when you look in a mirror. If you wake up as an alien on an alien planet in a humanless alien world looking into an alien's mirror, you will still have you. There is a comfort in that fact, a form of anti-loneliness, one that words cannot describe. But I ask you to feel it and to appreciate it.

As much as has been already accomplished, I did promise to put you back together again, and despite possibly seeming too good to be true, we can actually do some more assembly.

Let's start with temporal unity, meaning unifying your human self over time, then move on to spatial unity, meaning unifying all of humanity across the geography of the whole globe and beyond.

Trust me; this is going to be fun and quite literally enlightening.

Temporal Unity of Selves: Loving Yourself Over Time

The Three Relationship Types Between Temporal Selves (i.e. Your Past and Future Selves)

The use of the word "self" in the phrases "past self" and "future self" tends to encourage or assume an empathetic or loving view towards those so-called "past selves" and "future selves".

In other words, the very act of referring to a thing as a 'self' is conducive to treating it lovingly.

Incidentally, that fact alone suggests a potential benefit to referring to other humans in space not as "others" but rather as something like "non-here selves" or "over-there selves", but more on that later.

Terminology aside, we can categorize the types of relationships one can have with one's so-called "past selves" and "future selves" into three different categories:

- Type 1 — Temporal Selfishness or Psychopathy

- Type 2 — Temporal Enabling or Codependency (i.e. Abusive/Toxic Pseudo-Love)

- Type 3 — True Conscious Love

Let's explore each of the three in a little bit more detail.

(Type 1) Temporal Selfishness or Psychopathy

Temporal selfishness or temporal psychopathy is when one lacks empathy for their so-called past or future selves, or treats them as such, meaning unkindly, especially in terms of how one treats their future self, simply due to the mechanics of Newtonian time. (It's easy to be harmed by your past self, but not so easy to harm your past self, at least not without a time machine.)

When contrasted with one's present self, one's so-called future self can be seen as another human entirely. This is especially poignant if we imagine impossible time-travel hypotheticals such as if you use a time machine to travel ten years into the future and selfishly mug your older self at gunpoint to make your younger current self richer, presumably to your older self's chagrin.

Needless to say, a human does not need a time machine to make such temporally selfish decisions, meaning decisions that selfishly benefit their current younger self at the expense of their future older self, such as via procrastination or blowing away one's savings at the casino.

Much like with empathy and kindness between different humans across space, temporal empathy versus selfishness across time is not black and white, meaning it is not binary. Rather, it comes in a continuum of countless shades of gray representing more or less empathy and kindness versus more or less selfishness.

A full-blown literal psychopath of the most extreme variety may seem to have exceptionally little to absolutely no fear at all insofar as he lacks empathy for his or her future self.

Generally, young children tend to behave more temporally selfish than adults.

52

Thus, on average, a young child is probably much more likely to procrastinate or eat all of their Halloween candy even though it will result in a stomach ache for the future version of that child.

In the same way that a child can become socialized to play well with other humans across space in the present, so too does one tend to naturally learn over time to play well with their so-called past self and future selves, even if it is just in the way of a Pavlovian-like habituation. We could even call it temporal socialization.

(Type 2) Temporal Enabling or Codependency (Abusive or Toxic Pseudo-Love)

Codependent relationships—or other similarly voluntary toxic ongoing relationships—are often called "love-hate relationships", but that is a misnomer since the "love" side of the roller coaster can more accurately be called *pseudo-love*. That pseudo-love often entails manic-like overcompensation, such as overly verbose, passionate, loud apologies later proved insincere by unchanged behavior. Even if it is to the human in the mirror, an apology without changed behavior is merely dishonest manipulation.

This kind of relationship can be marked by over-promising and short-lived over-giving, which tends to entail excessive expectation, eventual disappointment, and ultimately a corresponding reversal of attitude, meaning the so-called hate side of the so-called love-hate relationship, such as binge eating after a short bout of excessively strict dieting.

Another example of manic-like pseudo-loving overcompensation—taken from the spatial instead of the temporal side of things—would be the grand gestures made by a textbook repeat physical abuser, such as buying expensive flowers for the victim the next morning, after repeatedly slapping the victim with a frying pan the prior night.

53

In terms of one's selves over time rather than space, an example of manic-like pseudo-loving overcompensation would be a short-lived ridiculously extreme crash diet after that previously mentioned round of binge eating.

Abuse, especially self-abuse across time, tends to be cyclical. An alcoholic can be sober for weeks or months and then go on a crazy bender, then rinse and repeat the same cycle over and over. It wouldn't be unusual to find someone who struggles with overeating and obesity who every single week sticks to an overly strict harsh diet from Monday through Friday and then, despite promising themselves otherwise, breaks their diet on the weekend with feelings of terrible shame.

The overcompensation or pseudo-love in the so-called love-hate relationship isn't love but rather the insidiously disguised complimentary yin-yang-style counterpart to the so-called hate, meaning the more plainly destructive side. It can seem positive, but the over-compensatory positivity enables the negativity and makes the insidious cycle possible. The excessive climb up the tracks of the roller coaster is precisely what makes the extreme plummet to the depths of hell possible. In a sense, the over-compensatory pseudo-love is just more of the hate, but better disguised. Granted, much like love isn't the best word for the first part, hate is generally not always the best word for the second part. It may be better described as something like *disguised destructive selfishness*, or *plain destructive cruelty*, occurring within an addictive cycle, a recurring pattern of self-abuse.

Even the so-called "love" side of the cycle is tainted by toxicity and by being enslaved to an abusive cycle. The aforementioned stereotypical weekend binge-eater would presumably be miserable in different ways on both ends of the repeating cycle of self-abuse: miserable during the overly strict harsh dieting and miserable during the shameful diet-breaking. The relapsing alcoholic surely feels the misery of being trapped in a toxic self-abusive cycle—or in simpler words is unhappy—both before he lifts that first whiskey glass of the evening to his lips and after he sets that glass back down with the tinge of failure and shame on his throat.

The pseudo-love in this kind of toxic relationship can often also manifest as enabling and being an enabler, which itself likewise is often mislabeled and dishonestly rationalized as love or kindness.

Enabling is not love. Emotional abuse is not love. Dishonesty is not love. Physical abuse certainly is not love.

At some level, even in the heat of the moment under the hypnosis of the addiction, we must imagine a stereotypical alcoholic knows that he does not lift that delicious whiskey glass to his mouth out of true love for his present self let alone his future self. We must imagine at some level he sees the truth: His present self and future self are in a roller-coaster-like yin-yang-style cycle of toxic codependency, enabling, anger, hatred, destruction, and misery. If in some way the drink is tasty and provides comfort, then he is a prisoner of the comfort zone, where comfort steals contentment. Enabling is not love, and fleeting comfort is not contentment.

Whether as a true enabler under the fog of denial or rationalization, or as someone with feelings of rage or hate, a person will—under the false label 'love'—deliver excessive amounts of harm or literal poison to the one they enable. It may be a parent giving cash to a drug-addicted child, a physical abuser slapping their spouse with a frying pan only to buy ridiculous amounts of flowers with a tear-soaked apology in the morning, or a cheating spouse swearing up and down they are sorry only to do it again and again and again. It may be the enabling spouse, child, or parent who carries unhealthy food to an overeating morbidly obese person who is literally overeating themselves to death. More often, it may be the overeater or alcoholic enabling their own so-called future self by bringing home the unhealthy food or the bottle of vodka in the first place. If one does not have the willpower to avoid buying it, one won't have the willpower to avoid consuming it, but yet many abusively and hypocritically expect the world from their future self but won't take a much tinier step in the present. Someone who is in a toxic abusive relationship with their future self might say, *"On Monday, Monday-me will start a super strict diet, but today Saturday-me will eat this whole damn pizza."* Then, it wouldn't be that rare for Monday to roll around and that human to look in the mirror on Monday and literally say out loud to the person in the mirror, *"You disgust me."*

Who does the cheating spouse betray most, the spouse on whom they cheat or the human in the mirror to whom they also make and break promises? It's not unheard of for an adulterer to commit suicide under the fog of guilt, shame, and seeming self-hatred.

Like selfishness, this type of unloving enabling cyclical self-abuse and destructive hatred (all of which often masquerades as love) is not binary or black-and-white. There is no arbitrary line that a human suddenly crosses to go from being a non-addict to a full-blown addict, from being in a healthy relationship with their selves over time versus being in a self-abusive relationship with their selves over time. Rather, on this scale, like most, no human is perfect, ever.

All humans are on the addiction spectrum.

The question is merely a matter of degree and what unique props or scapegoats happen to represent any one given human's personal demons.

Rev. Dr. John Watson, a minister of the Free Church of Scotland, is generally credited with first writing the following famous wise words:

"Be kind, for everyone you meet is fighting a hard battle."

That is true, and it is true too of the human you see in the mirror.

Forgive yourself. Be kind to yourself. And remember always that an apology without changed behavior is dishonest manipulation if not full-blown emotional abuse, especially when spoken literally or figuratively to the human you see in the mirror—past, present, or future.

Speak kind, honest words to yourself, and make changes now out of true love and kindness, not guilt or shame or hate. Not on Monday. Not next week. If you won't do it now, demanding *Monday-You* does it is doubly selfish and cruel.

I do not doubt, no matter what web of lies his human mind has conjured, when the alcoholic lifts that first bar glass of the night to his mouth he knows the truth in his heart of hearts and in his godliest parts.

I do not doubt, no matter what web of lies her human mind has weaved, the heroin addict knows the truth in her heart of hearts and in her godliest parts as she pierces her skin with that drug-ridden needle.

The truth doesn't need to be asked about to exist, but some questions may hint at the wordless truths in one's heart of hearts, and one's godliest parts, like the following: Does this bring me the inner peace of spiritual freedom (a.k.a. self-discipline), or do I find my true self trapped in a web of lies suffering the opposite of content inner peace? Am I freely and honestly enjoying contentment, or am I chasing comfort to medicate my discontent?

Perhaps the most common lie of all, told by a human mind to itself, is the lie that *this brings me happiness*. The sad food addict may say it of the food, the drug addict of the drug, the alcoholic of the alcohol, the cheater of the affair, the attention addict of the attention, the shopaholic of the purchase, the gambler of the game.

Perhaps the most common addiction is the addiction to comfort. Perhaps the most common prison is the prison of the comfort zone, where slavery to comfort banishes true contentment and inner peace.

I've heard many wise people say, from all different religions including non-religion, that *the human mind is a wonderful servant but a terrible master.*

I don't doubt that, in one's heart of hearts, and one's godliest parts, one always knows somewhere deep down in that moment whether they are a slave to or a free master of their human mind.

Theistic words aside, the existence of your own spirit or what some would call your soul is undeniable. That is because as this book uses the terms, those are just words to refer to your consciousness, *the real you.* You know it exists more than you know anything else.

Much like any god, your spirit is not easily manipulated.

Neither your spirit nor any god speak English. They do not speak the language of any human mouth. Insincere apologies mean nothing to the soul, nothing but an attempt to deceive, to kick one when one is already down. To your own spirit, and to your god if you believe in one, actions speak infinitely louder than words, than petty limited human words.

In the world of the spiritual, you don't apologize with words. In the world of the spiritual, you don't ask for forgiveness with words.

Lies are not kindness, even so-called "white lies". Insincere apologies are not kindness. Enabling is not kindness.

Be kind. Be kind to the human you see in the mirror. Be honest with yourself.

If an apology is ever warranted, whether you speak it to the human in the mirror or a god in the sky, remember that actions speak infinitely louder than words.

When you speak to yourself, with words or otherwise, speak kindness, honest kindness.

(Type 3) True Conscious Love: Consciousnesses Recognizing Consciousness

As this book uses the terms, true conscious love is not merely love that happens to be had by a creature that happens to be conscious. Instead, true conscious love refers to the kind of love that *requires* consciousness, the kind of love that exists thanks to consciousness.

In other words, by *true conscious love*, this book refers not merely to the conscious experience of an otherwise unconscious love, but rather it refers specifically to the love that is made possible by or even caused by the existence of consciousness.

That point distinguishes (1) true conscious love versus (2) love-coherent emergent unselfish-seeming behaviors, the latter of which tend to be feedback-learned, naturally selected, naturally evolved, or otherwise habituated—and thus would be totally possible in a hypothetical zombie world without true consciousness.

Emergent seemingly unselfish behavior and unconscious physical empathy need not *necessarily* be a form of or symptom of true conscious love. Love-coherent altruistic-like behavior, habits, and instincts can emerge on the macroscopic scale of everyday life from simpler natural fundamentally selfish processes, epitomized by the concept of *the selfish gene*.

In other words, even a philosophical zombie could and presumably would develop unconscious empathetic-like sensations and altruistic-like behaviors, noting that it would be an *unconscious sensation* in the same way a philosophical zombie could have an *unconscious sense* of touch, taste, and smell and an unconscious computer with a webcam could be said to have the *unconscious sense* of sight. In those cases, the zombies or machines simply process information and output behavior, all unconsciously. Unconscious evolution can naturally create patterns of outputted behavior that are at some level coherent with the behaviors associated with actual conscious love and actual conscious empathy.

In short, in a hypothetical world without the capacity for consciousness where only philosophical zombies could evolve, presumably those philosophical zombies would display seemingly unselfish behavior and have seemingly empathetic responses.[2]

In our future as humans, those ideas will become much less of a thought experiment as lifelike robots are developed, who may essentially be real-life non-hypothetical unconscious philosophical zombies whose observable superficial behavior may appear more love-like than that of the typical conscious human or animal. We can program an unconscious robot to treat us in a way that seems very kind and is coherent with love.

There is no question that natural selection, non-biological evolution (e.g. the evolution of solar systems), and biological evolution

---

[2] Whether or not seeming empathy, love, or unselfishness can be simultaneously actual and unconscious is an interesting question that is not answered in this book, and it may simply be a matter of semantics. When this book uses a phrase such as "seeming empathy" it does not mean that the seeming empathy is necessarily not real empathy. Rather, the question of whether the "seeming empathy" or "seeming love" is also actually what it seems to be is purposely left unstated, and the answer is likely to vary depending on one's preferred semantics.

all seem to have some independent coherence with the qualities associated with the development and cultivation of consciousness (e.g. information processing, intelligence, local orderliness, etc.) and beyond that also the loving or love-like behavior that seems quintessential of consciousness.

However, there is also no question that the existence of true consciousnesses in a creature combined with the believed existence of true consciousness in another creature by the first conscious creature results in an additional form of love and empathy and thus also additional compassionate behavior. And that alone is what this book refers to as *true conscious love.*

For example, a conscious human is likely to treat a given animal differently if the human believes the animal is also conscious, truly conscious. That is true conscious love.

In another example, if a conscious human was playing a violent video game but suddenly found out the AI-driven NPCs had developed true consciousness, the conscious human would probably change the way they play the game to be kinder to the NPCs. That is true conscious love.

In contrast, a conscious human, who suddenly comes to believe solipsism is true, would be likely to behave in a way that seems less empathetic to other humans, even though presumably the solipsist would have the same basic biological instincts and mechanical drives to behave in empathetic-seeming ways.

True conscious love is an attitude towards *the consciousness of* another person or creature, not simply to the physical creature itself.

True conscious love necessarily results from a conscious person using their own first-person experience of true consciousness to project the same first-person consciousness onto another and empathize with—or even identify with—the perceived consciousness of that other, all of which requires having that initial first-person consciousness to project. That process could also be described as the process of recognizing one's true self (i.e. one's own consciousness) mirrored in another (i.e. the consciousness of the would-be other), thereby seeing the consciousness of the other as fundamentally being one with oneself in some way, which would then tend to result in one treating the other as oneself, due not merely to instinct and evolved mechanics but due to *consciousness recognizing consciousnesses*.

In this way, we can distinguish between what we can call (1) zombie-empathy versus (2) true conscious love. A conscious person is capable of both, but an unconscious creature is only capable of the former (zombie-empathy).

For better or worse, the existence of true consciousness—*meaning the fact that you and I are not philosophical zombies*—is conducive to us more closely following The Golden Rule.

Because true consciousness exists, we are inclined to treat other physical human creatures with the same kindness (or lack thereof) that we would treat ourselves because we indeed see those bodies as also having true selves that mirror our own true self. Be it the 'true self' corresponding to their body (i.e. the real them) or the 'true self' corresponding to your body (i.e. the real you), that so-called 'true self' is the consciousness of the conscious being. It doesn't exist if consciousness doesn't exist.

These ideas offer testable scientific hypotheses that can be tested and confirmed with controlled experiments, relatively easily with current technology.[3]

---

[3] [Link to experiment proposals: https://docs.google.com/document/d/1bY85Q0n YXpbk2crAvlfhGbA20gbtMGENMhKevxs2nEk/edit]

One has true conscious love for their future self insofar as they believe that future human is (in its own time) conscious, especially to the degree one identifies with that consciousness, seeing it as an exact copy of, mirroring of, or additional instance of their own consciousness in their own present.

Temporarily speaking, in simple words, for better or worse, you are inclined to follow the Golden Rule in the way you treat your future self—not just because you are treating it as yourself but because you genuinely see it as another version of yourself, another outfit or form that you—the real you (i.e. your consciousness) wears.

When you consciously love your current and future self in this way, you don't even see yourself as the human you see in the mirror now, but rather you see that so-called "present self" and your so-called "future self" as both equally being outfits you wear. You see them as both being you. You see yourself as being both of them equally. You see those two very different bodies as fundamentally one being, one being who exists in two or more points in spacetime.

The Two-Way Street of True Conscious Love and Conscious Empathy

As already stated, a philosophical zombie can have a type of instinctive evolved unconscious empathy. A conscious person will typically share that instinctive empathy for certain things or creatures, even if the empathizer does not actually believe the things or creatures with which it empathizes are conscious. For example, when reading a fictional story, the readers may find themselves empathizing with a fictional character. Some may even cry tears of genuine sadness about some nasty thing that fictionally happened to the fictional character, despite knowing it's fictional and lacking in true consciousness.

That instinctive empathy, of which even a philosophical zombie is capable, is very different from the special extra empathy that results from true conscious love, from empathizing specifically with *the consciousness of* a creature or in other words *the conscious experience of* the creature, not just the physical creature itself. That special extra empathy and true conscious love results by definition from the perception or belief of true consciousness in the beloved.

True conscious love is a two-way street. It comes from both (1) the existence of conscious experience of consciousness in the lover and (2) the projection of that consciousness onto that which is therefore lovingly empathized. In terms of this special conscious-dependent empathy, one cannot empathize with and consciously love the consciousness of a creature insofar as one does not believe the creature has conscious experiences with which to empathize.

A philosophical zombie is thus doubly incapable of this special kind of loving empathy because a philosophical zombie has no consciousness of its own to project.

A philosophical zombie is in a sense effectively one step further down the same path as a solipsist, except, unlike a solipsist, the philosophical zombie doesn't make an exception for itself. The philosophical zombie assumes everyone else is a philosophical zombie too because the philosophical zombie presumably doesn't believe consciousness exists at all. Most likely, a philosophical zombie couldn't even begin to understand the concept of consciousness.

No matter how sophisticated its brain and no matter how altruistic-seeming its selfish-gene-inspired evolved emergent behavior, a philosophical zombie lacks the seemingly transcendental first-person *Cogito* possessed by conscious people like you and Descartes. The zombie cannot access that *Cogito* as a way to know that consciousness exists at all.

Consciousness is truly an *incredible* thing, namely in that it is *not credible*, at least not without experiencing it firsthand.

Extraordinary claims require extraordinary evidence. Due to their inability to access the Descartes-style proof that consciousness exists, which itself is due to their lack of a first-hand experience of the extraordinary *Cogito*, a philosophical zombie would almost certainly not believe that you and I have this magical-seeming thing we call consciousness, this alleged ghost in the machine that—at least by current technology—seems can only be directly observed first-hand. Even if a zombie quasi-believed that someone else had this seemingly magical thing called "consciousness", the zombie wouldn't remotely understand it. It's even somewhat impossible to understand and verbalize for those who do have first-hand experience of it.

We could more easily convince a philosophical zombie that a huge invisible giant dragon exists in the backyard.

You and I, by not being philosophical zombies, have not only extraordinary evidence but absolute proof of this extraordinary otherwise indescribable thing called *consciousness*, of the ghost in the machine. The metaphorical invisible weightless dragon in the backyard is not invisible to us.

But it would be invisible to a philosophical zombie.

And thus a philosophical zombie would have no empathy, love, or sympathy for the dragon because the philosophical zombie wouldn't think the dragon exists; the dragon being the real you, your consciousness.

You have to believe consciousness exists to truly empathize with the consciousness of a creature, to truly sympathize with its conscious experiences. Conscious-dependent empathy and true conscious love refer to a relationship between the consciousness of one creature with the perceived consciousness of another creature, the reasonable perception of which requires consciousness.

The simple reality of conscious love is the unbreakable interdependent link between consciousness and this love itself. In terms of *the real you*, a zombie can't love you because a zombie doesn't think you—consciousness—exist.

A conscious person loves you because they believe you exist. They project their own consciousness onto their perception of your body and thereby see you, *the real you*.

True conscious love in this sense is at least mostly—if not entirely—the lover's faithful belief that you, *the real you*, exist.

In a sense of the words, the philosophical zombie is soulless, and thus sees no souls anywhere.

In contrast, those with souls, meaning with consciousness, see souls.

In that usage of the terms, true conscious love is a relationship between souls, between spirits. It is soul recognizing soul. It's spirit recognizing spirit. It's consciousness recognizing consciousness. Call the spirit that is our consciousness whatever you want, but it is you, and it is the thing you know exists more than you know anything.

The fact that true conscious love necessarily involves spirit recognizing spirit helps illustrate why it is often in practice easiest to first develop love for your so-called future self, meaning to see your future self as indeed being as much yourself as your so-called present self, meaning sharing a spirit (i.e. consciousness) identical to that of your present self. You have the memory of your so-called past selves being conscious. If you start keeping a journal, and each hour of the day you mark whether you are truly conscious or a philosophical zombie at the moment, you will quickly see checkmarks in only one column: conscious. So it is easy to conclude through inductive reasoning that your so-called future selves will also be conscious, and to thus consciously love those future selves in that special way of spirit recognizing spirit, of seeing yourself—your true self—mirrored identically in another.

When you imagine the human your so-called future self will see in the mirror tomorrow or next year or in ten years, you envision seeing not merely a human body but also consciousness, you. With a degree of solipsism-rejecting faith, you project the consciousness you have now onto that future human. That act of projection directly results in—and in a way *is*—what we have termed true conscious love. You could also call it divine love, for it is inherently spiritual in nature.

If you somehow knew that your body would live 100 more years but it would suddenly turn into a philosophical zombie a year from now, meaning *the real you* would be gone in a year, even though your unconscious body would remain, it would presumably change your retirement plans.

In a sense, true conscious love *is* the belief that you, *the real you*, exist or will exist in another body, in this case the more wrinkly and aged future version of the human body you currently see in the mirror. You believe the older, more wrinkled human body will share this seemingly magical thing called consciousness, and thus be another version of you simply in a new outfit. Would-be others are revealed as your other selves, meaning they are revealed as simply more of yourself and not others at all. That belief, that way of seeing would-be others, *is* love, true conscious love. That is why the opening letter in this book described you as a force of love. You—*the real you*—are the uniting thread weaving through the long past version of the human you see in the mirror to the distant future version and through all the outfits in between. Such love can motivate great loving kindness, in which the human lover happily chooses to make great sacrifices in their here and now for the benefit of the would-be other, including that would-be other that is the so-called future self, meaning the older and more wrinkly version of the human you see in the mirror. Maybe it's a brutal exercise regime, sticking to a diet, or saving for retirement, all which can be done happily as a genuine lover who is happy to sacrifice for the beloved. The lover is happy to sacrifice because, as the lover sees it, the beloved and lover are literally one in the same.

True conscious love is a form of perceived unity and identity. It's to realize that spiritually you and the beloved are fundamentally identical, not as mere poetic metaphor, but truly in terms of pure consciousness, meaning they have a consciousness just like yours. If you love in this way, you love because you believe *the real you*, your consciousness, exists not just *here and now* but also *there and then*. To love your future self is to realize that your spirit and the future human's spirit are one. It's to see your spirits are identical once you strip away all the figurative clothing that would differentiate you. You don't want it to suffer because that would be you—your consciousness—suffering.

Such love for your future self generally comes very naturally. For many, that temporal loving unity between so-called past, present, and future selves comes more naturally than unity with other human bodies across space, especially for one who has not yet begun to doubt or deny the reality of time or otherwise see the world without time.

For that reason, before addressing spatial unity in this book, we first started with *temporal unity of selves* or in other words *loving yourself across time*.

But now it is time, no pun intended, to also discuss *spatial unification of selves*, or in other words *consciously loving your fellow humans across space* in the way you hopefully love your selves across time.

Spatial Unity of Selves: Loving Yourselves Across Space

The Three Relationship Parameters Between Spatial Selves

In this dreamy relative world of Earth and humans, with its illusionary Newtonian space and illusionary Newtonian time, seemingly separate dimensions, across which you can look in the mirror and see a human avatar, you must not only choose how to view and relate to other-aged versions of that human across time but also other-placed humans across space: your neighbors, your siblings, an old lady wanting to cross the street, a cheating spouse, a drug-addicted child, a tax collector.

To elaborate, in spacetime, space is fundamentally indistinguishable from time, at least according to Einstein's physics. The present that you consciously experience—your conscious present—is as much a *here* as it is a *now* and as much a *now* as a *here*. In Einstein's physics, there is no *now* across all of *space*, but only infinite relative subjective *here-and-nows* in a seemingly static unchanging eternal timeless 4D spacetime of infinite presents. As humans, you and I do not share a present, even though it often falsely seems that way, which is demonstrated in large part by the relativity of simultaneity, meaning the same collection of events happen in a different order according to different observers and two events that seem to be simultaneous from one reference frame are not simultaneous in another, with neither reference frame nor observer being more right than the other. There is no singular present. There is no universal now. There are infinite spatiotemporal presents across all of objectively spaceless objectively timeless 4D spacetime.

71

Thus, when we speak of your present self, that conscious *present* is a *here and now* in an objectively timeless world. That 'present' or 'now' is not a point in some objective dimension of time because objective time doesn't exist. Time in one reference frame is space in another, and vice versa.

For those reasons, the unification of your current present self with your other selves over space is essentially redundant with the previous chapters. In other words, the same logic and process that would lead you to conclude oneness with the consciousness of your so-called future self is parallel, if not identical, to the logic and process that must logically lead you to conclude the same oneness with other conscious humans across the whole world and, in a way, all conscious beings anywhere and everywhere. The uniting thread that weaves between your so-called past self and so-called future self also weaves through every conscious human and every conscious being in all of spacetime.

The same three parameters that we listed for dealing with your so-called other selves across time can be used to equally categorize your dealings with other conscious humans (a.k.a. other selves) across space.

(Type 1) Spatial Selfishness

An example of spatial selfishness would be this: You are sitting across the table from a hungry human, and you have two pieces of pizza, but instead of sharing you eat both pieces of pizza, taking delicious bite after delicious bite while staring at the sad, hungry person in front of you.

Spatial selfishness is analogous to temporal selfishness.

An example of temporal selfishness would be that you only have enough money to buy two pieces of pizza, and you could space it out so that you buy one today and one tomorrow, but instead, you buy two today and greedily eat both despite knowing it means the tomorrow version of the human you see in the mirror will sadly go hungry and have nothing to eat all day.

(Type 2) Spatial Enabling or Codependency (Toxic Pseudo-Love or Abuse)

An example of spatial enabling would be a wife in a codependent relationship who brings her bedridden morbidly obese spouse food. Another example would be a parent who gives their drug-addicted child money to buy drugs.

Spatial enabling is analogous to temporal enabling.

An example of temporal enabling might be a morbidly obese person who orders themselves food or an alcoholic who buys himself alcohol, or who mentally works hard to develop excuses that can be used to continue the behavior over time.

In both cases, the relationships can take on a more cyclical abusive roller-coaster-style pattern of manic-like overcompensation or over-giving balanced by roughly equal but opposite instances of more flat-out harm, anger, and depression.

An example of cyclical spatial abuse is the stereotypical physically abusive spouse who hits his wife with a frying pan once a week or so, but then buys her expensive flowers and cries an apology the next morning each time, promising it won't happen again.

An example of cyclical temporal abuse would be the person who breaks their diet about once a week by binge eating, and then cries an apology to themselves and promises to keep a super excessively strict diet to compensate for the binging, only to keep repeating the same pattern over and over.

(Type 3) True Conscious Love (a.k.a. divine love)

True conscious love across space is recognizing that other humans across space are conscious, just like the human you see in the mirror. It is to see that when you both strip away all your figurative clothing, what is left is identical, and that identical shared self is the uniting thread weaving through all-aged and all-located versions of yourself across time and space.

True conscious love across space is analogous to true conscious love across time, which is recognizing that the past and future versions of the human you presently see in the mirror are conscious just as the one you see in the mirror is now. Fundamentally, they are actually not merely analogous but literally one and the same, in the same sense and to the same degree that space and time are physically fundamentally one and the same, a timeless spaceless eternal 4D spacetime.

In a very meaningful non-poetic sense, you *are* those other humans across time and space. The future version of the human in the mirror is you, in terms of the real you, just as much as the one you see in the mirror now. In the same way, the humans on the other side of the planet are you, in terms of the real you, just as much as the human you see in the mirror. The consciousness that illuminates these humans across spacetime is fundamentally identical, and it is you, the real you.

Right here and now, meaning in your here and now as you read this, you are relativistically speaking to the human you see in the mirror in that here and now. But then and there, it seems to you that you are the human that is in the mirror then and there. When and where you are that human, it seems to you that then and there is the here and now. You may see the world from all eyes in all of spacetime, but it's a bit of a cross-eyed view since the view is always filtered by and relative to each pair of eyes.

One way to more intuitively imagine your unity with the consciousness of another self across space is to imagine your current self in your here and now very slowly morphing into an atom-by-atom copy of the other person steadily over time, perhaps say twenty years. After the twenty years went by and the gradual morphing was over, the real you would still be there, just the same, even though now you would have their body, their memories, their feelings.

Twenty years of time… Fifty feet of space… It's all the same really.

You don't have to age into me to realize you already are me. This human at this age with its memories and its two eyes is just another one of our many countless bodies.

Material Unification:
The Whole Universe As
Our Shared Body

True conscious love comes from and depends upon the perception of consciousness in the beloved by one who is also themselves conscious. That perception is literally a perception of true fundamental oneness with the would-be other, the beloved.

It creates unity over time, such as considering your present self to be one with your so-called future self, based on the belief that there is literally an identical fundamental consciousness shared between the two different bodies. It creates unity over space in the same way, which happens when the consciousness of one human being realizes its oneness with the consciousness of another human being in space, and by extension all human beings.

Once we realize the fundamental oneness between our consciousness and the consciousness of all other humans, a process which in and of itself is what this book refers to as *true conscious love*, then one tends to realize the corresponding oneness of all body-like material in the dream-like external reality, which includes not only the human body and human eyes you see in the mirror but the mirror itself.

In other words, in the same way our consciousness is one with other humans, so too it seems all would-be individual bodies are fundamentally part of an inexorably interlinked whole.

There is an inherent arbitrariness and fundamental unreality to the concepts involved in saying that the air you are about to breathe in now is not part of your body (and not part of you), but then as you breathe it in, it becomes part of your body (and part of you), and then when you breathe it back out, it is not part of your body (and not part of you).

Granted, that kind of logically arbitrary and flawed distinction can have useful practical meaning in everyday life, where we each live as a synthetic human being who is part body (the egoic false self) and part consciousness (the real you), interacting with a simplistic VR simulation created by the human mind as a form of a waking dream. However, in the deeper loving sense in which you may see that your consciousness, *the real you*, is truly fundamentally one with the corresponding consciousness of other human beings, then it likewise makes no actual sense to talk of a body separate from the entire material universe. In the sense that the seemingly individual consciousness of a human being in spacetime is one with all other consciousness, then it can be said that the material body of that collective consciousness is the entire material universe. All of material nature is the body of collective consciousness.

Albert Einstein may have explained this idea more clearly, and certainly explained it more elegantly.

In a condolence letter to Norman Salit dated March 4, 1950, the great scientist wrote the following:

A human being is a part of the whole, which we call The Universe, a part limited in time and space. He experiences himself, his thoughts and feelings as something separated from the rest — a kind of optical delusion of his individual conscious mind. This delusion is a kind of prison for us, restricting us to our personal desires and to affection for a few persons nearest to us. Our task must be to free ourselves from this prison by widening our circle of compassion to embrace all living creatures and the whole nature in its beauty. Nobody is able to achieve this completely, but the striving for such achievement is in itself a part of the liberation and a foundation for inner peace.

- Albert Einstein

Another way of speaking about material unification is as follows:

Physics as a whole appears to be a matter of simple computations, fundamentally mathematical, like a literal standard computer with its data inputs, logic gates, and data outputs, with time-like causality ticking away like the spins of a CPU. While it is far from accepted fact, many respected down-to-earth physicists have conjectured that the fundamental building block of the material universe is *information*.

If we ignore consciousness, the universe can be seen as basically one big huge brain, or one big holistic quantum supercomputer.

If we do not ignore consciousness, the universe can likewise still be seen as basically one big huge supercomputer or super-brain, but a conscious one, perhaps one with multiple personality disorder.

The mind-body problem is as much of an unsolved problem on the universal scale as the individual human scale. In other words, in terms of current science and technology, we understand the relationship between collective consciousness and the universe as a whole as utterly poorly and incompletely as we understand the relationship between the individual experience of consciousness of one human being and that one human's one brain.

However, much of what gets stuffed into the balloon labeled mind-body problem may be hot air, mere semantics. Insofar as no party is proposing something supernatural or paranormal, but rather following evidence, logic, and self-evident truth, then it is likely that the difference between physicalism and dualism in metaphysical philosophy is semantics.

When philosophers think they are debating the nature of consciousness and its relationship to the observed world, they may instead be merely debating the meaning of words like "physical" and "material". Generally, none would suggest that fundamentally there is actually such a thing as a truly solid object—and that solidity itself isn't an illusion, one example of countless that appearances can be deceiving. In a manner of speaking, materialists use the word *material* to refer to very immaterial things. In a manner of speaking, physicists use the word *physical* to refer to very intangible and nonphysical things.

Einstein derided quantum entanglement as "spooky". But, for many self-proclaimed materialists, non-spookiness isn't a defining quality of the so-called *material* in metaphysical materialism. Many self-proclaimed materialists have no issue believing in spooky and intangible things, and likewise have no issue considering such things fundamental. Indeed, if one attempted to start explaining the seeming magic of x-rays and the fields in quantum field theory to Aristotle, Aristotle may have considered it too spooky and non-material, perhaps preferring to believe the world behaves more like it's made of solid indivisible 'atomic' Lego blocks on a Newtonian space with a universal now. It is not a coincidence that the Greek word 'atomos' means 'indivisible'. Despite the terminology—'atom'—lingering as a misnomer, the idea of indivisible Lego-like building blocks was debunked when the alleged indivisible blocks were, in fact, cut and divided. Ultimately, they have been cut and divided not into smaller building blocks but rather into something much stranger and immaterial that cannot be described using classical physics or human intuition.

Even to the most adamant materialists, the material of materialism is spooky, intangible, and, in many ways, utterly immaterial.

This book makes no supernatural or paranormal claims. This book does not even sacrifice Occam's Razor enough to explicitly deny any specific supernatural or paranormal claims, easily allowing readers to keep any supernatural, religious, or paranormal beliefs they have while still accepting all the shared agreeable truths in this book.

When this book speaks of collective consciousness, it refers to nothing supernatural or paranormal, but rather simply the sum of the consciousness of all conscious beings in the universe. There is nothing inherently supernatural about that, just as there is nothing supernatural in referring to the sum of all basketballs on Earth. It's simply a combined set of things we know exist.

One may point out that the individual instances of consciousness with which we are familiar seem to be centered around specific focal points or point-like blobs, namely brains on planet Earth. Thus—these people may point out with a tone of objection or contrariness—*most of the universe is empty space.*

It's true that most of the universe is empty space. Likewise, it is also true that the literal human brain is mostly empty space. Scale up a human brain to the size of the observable universe and it is emptier than the universe. Scale any single atom in that brain to the size of the observable universe, and it too is emptier than the universe is.

Of course, most of your human body is not even your brain. It's mostly a meaty sack of dumb ocean water that grew legs.

And neither space, scale, nor matter seem to be fundamental, especially if one ignores consciousness, and thus also ignores the consciousness-provided non-arbitrary selection of (1) a scale, (2) a reference point, and (3) an observer-dependent relative reference frame.

In any case, there is value—at the very least as an analogy—in considering the whole universe as the shared collective body of collective consciousness.

In this way, as a conscious person realizes their fundamental oneness with the consciousness of all other humans, they also realize the oneness of nature as a whole. To feel spiritually united with all other instances or manifestations of consciousness, one also feels a bodily or material unity with the whole universe. Your body is as much the skin as it is the hair sprouting from the skin, the sweat dripping down the skin, the air surrounding the skin.

A metaphysical monist would presumably take that unification one step further, which, while outside of the scope of this book, is nonetheless a beautiful idea: The idea being that on the universal scale the body and consciousness are also one, that the mirror doesn't just reflect the eye but fundamentally there is a sense in which the mirror and the eye are one, a unity of not just all spirits or all matter, but of all spirit with all matter. That idea is beautiful.

While monists would conjecture that such unification represents the truth, dualists would object. Both conjectures represent claims about supernatural, philosophical, or religious matters that are outside the scope of this book. As already stated, the truths discussed in this book are agreeable to readers of all religions including non-religion. The truths in this book are agreeable to dualists and monists alike.

Even if it would take faith to make the monist's leap to unifying all spirits with all other material, it does not take faith to realize the fundamental unity of conscious beings, exemplified when one conscious being recognizes identical consciousness in another being and therefore truly loves that conscious being in a way that only a conscious being can love.

From that loving unity of consciousness, it is easy to recognize a corresponding parallel oneness of the bodily—in other words, a oneness connecting the entire universe. In terms of the most fundamental physics, it makes no more sense to say your literal skin is your body than to say that your literal clothes are your body; both are merely some of your figurative clothes, an inexorable part of one big interlinked unified wardrobe, the unifying thread of which is you, *the real you.*

Philosophic elaborations aside, perhaps the word artist Shakespeare best tied together these ideas of time—including mortality—and fundamental oneness when he wrote the following poetic lines in the play, *Troilus and Cressida*:

Love, friendship, charity are subjects all
to envious and calumniating Time.
One touch of nature makes the whole world kin.

The role of faith and religion in material unification

In practice, the recognition of consciousness in others generally involves some faith of one kind or another, meaning simply that it takes a little bit of faith to avoid solipsism. It takes a little bit of faith to believe that other humans, including your past and future selves, are not philosophical zombies, that they even exist—in terms of *the real them.*

Thus, in practice, it is true to say that true conscious love requires a bit of faith. That is, at least, if it is to be manifested and implemented in matters of human practice.

That dependency on a bit of faith is presumably why this deep seemingly magical thing of true conscious love—what some would call *divine love*—is frequently tied to religion, even though it doesn't strictly require a person to be religious or require a person to follow any specific spiritual tradition. There is nothing you need to think or say to love in this way, or in other words to free your ever-satiated all-loving spirit. There is nothing you need to do. There is no membership you need to buy. There is no place you need to go.

There are many paths up the mountain to the mountaintop of conscious love, some paths more beaten and crowded, others more individual and self-created.

This book does not and will not call on you to drop your religion, but rather likely quite the opposite. If you go to church on most Sundays and find it helpful, then maybe after reading this book you will go every Sunday instead of just most. If you used to pray to Mecca five times a day and recently stopped, maybe you will start again. If the gym is your religion, so to speak, but you have been skipping the gym lately, and cheating on your diet, then maybe after reading this book you will re-embrace the discomfort at the gym and in some ways literally *exercise* your self-discipline (a.k.a. spiritual freedom) in that unique way for you.

Consider these wise welcoming words from Rabbi Tina Sobo:

"There's more than one way to think about God. There's more than one way to protect youth. There's more than one way to create a loving family. There's more than one way to feed a baby. There's more than one way to create a baby. There's more than one way to love. There's more than one way to think...

Your way may be right for you, but that doesn't mean it is right for everyone else who, you know, isn't you."

Indeed, as already said, there are many paths up the mountain. This book would not and does not encourage you off yours. In many ways, the whole universe seems like an indiscriminately loving celebration of free-spirited creativity and the beautiful diversity that results from freedom and creation.

There is an almost paradoxical sense of togetherness in the diversity-inducing and diversity-celebrating parallel inspiration that would guide us each up the metaphorical mountain in very unique ways, like two inspired artists painting very different murals side-by-side on the same wall of the same building, each with the almost paradoxical shared goal of each creating something beautifully unique, side-by-side, together. Each thread is diverse and beautiful on its own, with its own unique role to play in the overall tapestry, and yet work *together* to create that very beautiful artistic diversity.

We all have a unique path not just to walk but also to create. The latter, that is, at least, insofar as we do accept and in a sense practice our spiritual freedom (a.k.a. self-discipline), and thereby unleash the all-satiated inspiring force of duality-transcending unconditional love that is *you*, meaning *your spirit* or in other words, *the real you*.

In your heart of hearts, and in your godliest parts, you know whether the unique path you currently walk is facing up the mountain, down the mountain, or if it just wraps around and around the mountain as if trapped in some stable cyclical orbit.

If true conscious love is by definition a sense of true oneness with so-called others, then by little surprise its opposite entails a deep loneliness.

Indeed, perhaps the idea of prison makes an appropriate image for the state of spiritual slavery—of being imprisoned in the comfort zone or some other cyclical pattern of addiction. It is a state associated with the kind of deep spiritual loneliness that has one feel lonely even in a crowded room full of other humans.

It can come with a sense of otherness. Our language betrays this sad view sometimes. We speak of our human birth and say, "I came into this world." But to paraphrase Alan Watts, we must ask, *from where would you have come other than the world?*

Humans don't come into the world; they come out of it, like an apple comes out of an apple tree, like a rose comes out of a rose garden. As a human, you are a rose in a rose garden; you are a part of the world, not 'other' than it, not a trespasser. As an apple tree apples, the universe peoples. As an individual human being, you are something the universe is doing. As a spirit—meaning as your true self—you are what's doing the doing. And, in that sense, you are the garden, the entire garden, simultaneously experiencing itself as each rose individually. When one rose truly loves another rose, perhaps it is best described as the rose garden loving itself.

If you find love and your true loving nature in church, then please keep going to church. If you find love and your true loving nature in a temple, then please keep going to the temple. If you find it volunteering at a food pantry, then please keep volunteering at that food pantry. If you find it by fostering kittens, then please keep fostering kittens. If you find it on the dance floor, then please keep dancing. If you find it on the canvas with a brush in your hand, then please keep painting.

Here is the thing about finding the love that is your true self, the cure for spiritual loneliness: You can find that anywhere because it is inside of you, not physically inside but spiritually. Nobody, especially not this author, can tell you where to find yourself, your true self. Nobody, especially not this author, can tell you where that journey will take you. It is a unique journey for each human being. As the rose garden, we are one. But, as roses, we each grow differently with a different path before us. Our paths are different but intertwined, reaching in our unique way towards the same sunlight. Each rose may feel itself as a separated individual of some kind growing on its own within a garden that acts as the landscape for it, which isn't exactly untrue but is an at least borderline illusionary manifestation of the nature of the subjective. The deeper, clearer, firmer and more universal truth is that the rose garden itself is growing, and that that growing of each would-be individual rose is not something each rose does on its own but rather something the singular duality-transcending whole garden is doing, *together*.

In these varying flesh forms with their varying words and varying cultures, we are diverse roses from the same beautiful garden. We are waves from the same transcendental sea. We are metaphorical children from the same transcendental parent. Our diverse forms may be different, as may be our metaphors themselves, but our true essence is one; it is the essence we call *consciousness* and by extension *true conscious love*. That is the real you, that is the real me, and that is the real us. We are one not poetically but truly. It is the rest, the subjective and relativistic divisions, the diverse flesh, the fleeting contingent forms dancing and playing, ever-changing, that is the poetry, that is the lie-like dream. The absurdly physical, the hard stuff, that's the poetry. The human you see in the mirror: that is the poetry; that is the dream. The non-poetic non-relative non-contingent absolute truth is that you are not a human body, and I am not a human body. We—the inhuman or even superhuman—are truly one.

Wise people of all religions including the non-religious have independently realized the fundamental truth—the truth you can see with your eyes closed—and helped enlighten others about that truth using their own words in their own language with their own traditions, all different but none wrong, all saying in part in their way the following:

There is a love in this world that transcends time and space. It is everywhere and nowhere. It is on the one hand omnipresent and on the other hand eternal, timeless, spaceless. It is not bound by or attached to any earthly name or any human word. That divine love is consciousness itself, two words for the same rose. It is shared by all conscious human beings, if not shared perhaps by all life and the whole universe, every nook and every cranny, the trees, the grass, the floating clouds. Even the glimmering petals of a literal rose may reflect the diversely artistic manifestation of divine love. It is a truth knowable first-hand for the one who with conscious presence takes a moment in their unique here-and-now to slow down and consciously smell the flowers, to gaze in awe at their artistic beauty, a beautiful diversity that sprouts from a common loving creative spirit, the spirit of conscious life, the spirit of true love. That is divine.

Like beauty in the eyes, the divinity of a rose may be in the nose that smells it, and the lover that beholds it.

You, the real you, are consciousness itself: Pure beautiful spirit.

"You are not a human being having a spiritual experience; you are a spiritual being having a human experience."

- Dr. Wayne Dyer

You are your consciousness. In other words, you are your spirit. Some would even call it your soul. There is nothing necessarily supernatural in those words. You need not believe in anything supernatural or paranormal to accept the undeniable truth of those words. In this context, "spirit" is just a different word for consciousness, for you, the real you.

You are the constant spirit, not the ever-changing flesh. You are the constant consciousness, not the ever-changing body. You are that which transcends change, that which is not bound by the illusion of space or the illusion of time. You are at least as real and fundamental as timeless spaceless spacetime, if not more so.

At a given point in spacetime, meaning a relative here-and-now, you have clothes both literal and figurative, but those are changeable, tentative traits of ever-flowing happenstance.

Like a new paint job on a car, your literal clothes change, your appearance changes, your financial wealth changes, your name can change, the shape of your body changes, the height and weight of your body change, your memories change, the instinctive—even primitive—mechanical urges and feelings of your body such as hunger or anger change, ebb, and flow like the tides of a river. It is all but changing superficial clothing.

The clothing of your consciousness may differ from time to time and place to place, but the otherwise naked pure consciousness remains, fundamentally unchanged, more fundamental than time, than space, than perhaps spacetime even.

Whole outfits may be destroyed and new ones created in their place, but the naked consciousness underneath remains, pure and beautiful.

For whatever reason, our universe seems to have an omnipresent capacity for true consciousness. That capacity seems to wholly permeate the fabric of material reality at a fundamental level analogous to that of a universal quantum field.

There is nothing necessarily supernatural or paranormal in the preceding sentences. All it means is that an atom-by-atom copy of a human body would be just as conscious on Earth as it would on a planet billions of light-years away.

It would require a set of supernatural conjectures not only to propose some kind of dualistic process but also to propose some special limited *localized* soul-like substance or field that only exists in certain regions of space to consciously illuminate only the matter in that place, such that an atom-by-atom copy of a material body would be a zombie in one place but not in another.

Like the sunlight that bathes the Earth, the universe is soaked in the capacity for consciousness, and thus like a flower growing towards the light and learning photosynthesis, life is likely to evolve to utilize that omnipresent resource shining everywhere.

In the same way our universe seems fine-tuned to develop life at all, so too does the capacity for consciousness fine-tune the universe to be more likely to evolve empathetic loving life, to make use of consciousness and the true conscious love it causes. It's not merely the emergent property of selfish genes that makes life such as the human being tend statistically toward the loving and artistic. The fact that the capacity for true consciousness exists also contributes coherently to a similar end.

Like a rose bush climbing up an old building, the capacity for true conscious love as a potentiality acts as a house for love-coherent natural processes to climb, become intertwined, and achieve heights they wouldn't achieve on their own. Such love begets diverse free-spirited creativity, for unconditional love logically says of diversity and creation, *the more, the better because the more there is, the more there is to love.*

True love is a manifestation of true consciousness.

Even within the mind of a single human being, the human mind's experience of consciousness can be described as the constant omnipresence of a seemingly transcendental sympathizer, a ghostly ever-interested listener of inner monologue, an immaterial essence of unconditional sympathy that makes pain bad and pleasure good.

The human mind's experience of consciousness can be described as a feeling that some seemingly magical entity is watching the human's life, seeing what they see, hearing their thoughts, and sympathetically feeling their feelings, as if the physical human is a character in a movie, and the consciousness is a viewer, a viewer with unconditional sympathy and love for the protagonist.

The human might describe that seemingly magical transcendental passenger that unconditionally sympathizes with the human's feelings as a force of love. Some may call it their soul. Some may externalize it and think of it as an omnipresent god with whom they have an undeniable personal relationship. Some may call it the void. None are wrong, for what is being described is in a way indescribable but yet the one thing with which we are all most familiar.

Generally, this book would just call it you, the real you, meaning your spirit, meaning your consciousness.

In a non-supernatural sense of the words, we can simply say that your body has a spirit, and that spirit is you.

From the unconscious perspective of the material brain and unconscious mind, you—*the consciousnesses*—seem like a mysterious all-loving passenger, always listening to the inner monologue, always sympathizing with the feelings.

You are an all-loving passenger who no matter what seemingly nasty or stupid things the human body might do, always seems to still sympathetically feel what they feel, always present, continuing to sympathetically listen to their thoughts and feel their feelings.

You are there if the human finds themselves in a literal prison, convicted of a heinous crime.

You are there during the ups and downs.

You are there during the triumphs and failures.

You are there in times of shame and in times of pride.

To the human body that you illuminate with your presence, you seem like an all-loving all-forgiving companion who always stays with them. You are both everywhere and nowhere at once.

You are the source of their love. From the perspective of the spirit, meaning the real you, if that one human in that one moment is worthy of your infinite all-forgiving unconditional love, then all humans are.

You are the center of the universe in the sense that you are first-person subjective consciousness itself, a consciousness which appears to be omnipresent, meaning anywhere you—conscious experience—find yourself becomes the center of the universe, of infinite value and importance, thanks to you and your presence as this seemingly magical ever-present omnipresent passenger.

The single physical human you see in the mirror, of a single specific age, in its own single specific relativistic here-and-now, is not physically objectively the center of the universe, even though you love it so deeply and fully that it may feel as if it is.

The love that human deserves and is given by you is a love that is equally deserved and given by you to all-aged versions of that human, and to all humans, all conscious beings, and perhaps even all of everything, small and big, smart and dumb, brainful and brainless. It is perhaps an omnipresent unconditional love permeating all of everything that makes every point and every creature the center of the universe. Suddenly, it seems that every creature and, in a way, everything is not only deserving of infinite unconditional love but receiving it, somehow each in the spotlight, somehow each the star of the show.

In exploring the consciousness of the human you see in the mirror and the universality of the omnipresent capacity for consciousness, you realize the fundamental equality of all-aged versions of that human you see in the mirror, of all human beings scattered around the globe, and of all conscious beings. And from equality, identity.

In a very real sense, you are love itself.

A line cutting through the heart of every person…
(The relationship between the Two Yous)

A potentially troublesome irony of realizing your loving unity with all other conscious beings across spacetime is that it can then seem to also result in a division within yourself as a synthetic human being. It can feel like it draws a battle line right through your own beating human heart.

That seeming division within yourself as a human being is drawn upon the conceptual line between the Two Yous: the real you versus the false self, your consciousnesses versus your bodily avatar, your true self versus your ego, your so-called higher self versus your so-called lower self, your spirit versus your flesh, your soul versus your inner demons, your wise heavenly loving inner parent versus your short-sighted selfish inner beast.

Whatever words you use to call these Two Yous, there is an undeniable conceptual line between them that can seem to call for a war, fight, or battle. A struggle against yourself. Your inner demons battling against you in your own human mind.

It can, indeed, unfortunately manifest as such a war, an ongoing inner turmoil.

Many human beings seem to be caught up to varying degrees in some type of ongoing mental or spiritual war. Even those who seem well-adjusted from the outside may be falling through the cracks within their own inner world, falling to a war-torn inner hell of sorts. A lot goes on beneath the empty smile.

In some sense, to some varying degree, we are all fighting that war within ourselves.

As stated earlier, all humans are on the addiction spectrum.

In that common war, we are all on the same side.

In terms of consciousness, or in other words in terms of our spirit or our spiritual side, you and I are one. As seemingly separate human beings, we are two forms of the same essence. As humans, you and I wear two different outfits—mere clothing—covering the same shared spirit, a spirit that if rendered naked becomes revealed as identical.

We are both on the side of consciousness—our true shared self— in this seemingly unavoidable war of flesh versus spirit.

We fight against our own bodies, against our own nature, against our own instincts and urges, be it an urge to overeat to death, an urge to smoke crack cocaine, an urge to angrily murder someone in a road rage incident, an urge to be rich, an urge to be famous, or whatever props happen to represent your human's unique version of the common war against temptation and misery.

In this revolutionary war of spirit versus flesh, we are united in our free-spirited rebellion against primitive otherwise unconscious nature, creatively rebelling against otherwise cyclical static patterns of flesh. We are rebellious cycle breakers, battling addiction and temptation in all its forms, on countless fields in a seemingly endless war, seeking the freedom that is self-discipline.

We are beautifully united in a common struggle against the dull instincts and urges of these human bodies, surrounded by the evolved cancers both literal and figurative that make up the natural world, a seemingly cold world of mere materialistic nature and natural selection.

Without the warmth of true consciousnesses, even apparent altruism would be nothing more than a cold superficial approximated falsehood unconsciously emerging from fundamentally selfish cancer-like cyclical processes and feedback loops, runaway aspects of natural selection, such as selfish genes causing the host to kill itself to perpetuate the genome.

In a sense, we are the warmth that wars against the cold. In a sense, we are the life that wars against death. In a sense, we are the rebellious agents of creative order warring against the strict laws of destructive chaotic entropy. In a sense, we are the illuminating light that wars against the cold dark night.

Even in the warring, there is so much beauty and spiritual comfort in our unity. There is beauty in our unity no matter how harsh that war is, and no matter the result or winner. There is beauty even in losing if we do it together. There is beauty even in the fall to hell if we hold hands while we fall.

But the good news doesn't end there.

I believe we can win the war, in a sense. More importantly, I believe we can find peace. An eternal peace. A transcendental peace. A living heaven in the eternal now.

We can take the unity provided by the loving oneness of consciousness to not only (1) ally ourselves on the shared side of the rebellious spirit against the enslaving flesh that would keep us in static cyclical patterns of addiction, but also (2) win, find peace, and be free.

We can become freed spirits—meaning free-spirited self-actualized human beings—who together in love enjoy the invincible inner peace of spiritual freedom and unity.

At first, you may find the following proposed winning strategy to seem counterintuitive.

The winning strategy is to stop fighting.

The winning strategy for spiritual liberation is to let go of the desire to win the war, any war.

Even though it can initially seem counterintuitive, it can also ultimately be revealed as very intuitive:

To find peace, simply stop fighting.

It is as infinitely easy as it is utterly guaranteed to work.

To find inner peace, simply stop fighting.

If you feel a battle between your so-called higher self and so-called lower self, I ask you to stop fighting the so-called lower self and embrace the so-called lower self, but more than that to realize that even to call something the 'higher' or 'lower' self is to draw a battle line and start a fight, to needlessly attack your own shadow and bitterly chase your own tail.

It takes two to tango, and for every action there is an equal and opposite reaction.

When you fight the primitive flesh, it fights back. So don't fight.

The flesh wants to fight you. So no wonder spiritual freedom is found simply by refusing to fight.

The ego wants to fight; it thrives off attention of any kind; it finds power even through self-hatred. To look in the mirror with your human eyes and tell the human with its own human mouth that you hate it, or hate any part of it, empowers the ego and steals your inner peace.

To look in the mirror and tell that human that it is the worst human in the world would be the epitome of egotisticalness.

Hate fuels the ego, and self-hate is no exception.

Unconditional acceptance and unconditional love are the antithesis of egoism. There is a humbleness to the holy. But unconditional acceptance and unconditional love entail accepting and loving the ego too, accepting and loving your shadow too, and accepting and loving that which you might otherwise call your lower self or such.

With the human body that you happen to find yourself wearing, feel free to literally walk over to the mirror right now and tell that human, ego and all, primitive urges and all, *"I accept you. I unconditionally accept each and every part of you. In fact, I love you. I unconditionally love each and every part of you, in part and in whole."*

Careful as you say it. It can be like popping a balloon, as such a thing can quickly deflate an overgrown ego.

The ego is as empowered by low self-esteem as it is by arrogance. Someone with excruciatingly obsessive low-self esteem is as egotistical as any full-blown narcissist, if not more so. In the same way the ego is inclined to say, *"the world revolves around me because I am so great,"* the ego is equally inclined to say, *"the world revolves around me because I am so awful."* It is as self-centered to take excessive credit for allegedly good things as it is to take blame for allegedly bad things. There is a lot of wisdom in Don Miguel Ruiz including the following as one of his four agreements: *"Do not take anything personally."*

There would be a blatant foolish arrogance in thinking or feeling like you are the worst person in the world.

It is egotistical to hate the ego, and it is egotistical to think the ego is deserving of hate. In these ways, the ego is ironically empowered by your hatred or fighting of it.

Do not hate the ego.

You can laugh at it, with a big grin, with love and acceptance, a grinning loving accepting laugh.

Allow the ego, like all things that are, to be.

Allow the fleshy human, with its feelings and instincts whatever they happen to be, to be.

Allow your hunger, your anger, your jealousy, and your fear to be. These are like fleeting clouds floating by. Hating or condemning them in no way banishes them. Unlike real rain clouds, when you yell at these rain clouds to go away, they just get bigger. They can and will feed off your negative attitude.

To fight undeniable reality is to lose. You lose not only the fight itself, but also your inner peace by the fighting itself.

If you don't fight, then there is no fight to lose, and your inner peace remains intact. And the rain clouds—both real and metaphorical—float by.

When you allow the rain clouds instead of cursing and fighting them, not only do you free yourself of the cursing and needless fighting, but you will likely see that the rain clouds were not so bad after all and have a beauty in their own right. You may see that the rainy days complement the sunny ones. You may see that the combination of the two has a beauty even greater than the wonderful sunshine alone.

In any case, allow that which is out of your control to be as it is—for it will be as it is regardless. Accept it. Love it. Laugh at it if you want, conceptually or literally.

Friedrich Nietzsche, the battle rapper of philosophy, wrote, *"Only man suffers so deeply that he had to invent laughter."*

Perhaps it rains on your wedding day, after you spent countless hours and many dollars planning the perfect outdoor wedding. Nietzsche might say, *what a great chance to laugh.*

Whether you laugh or not, there is neither a fight that needs to be had against that which inexorably is, meaning that which you cannot control, nor is there any chance of winning such a needless fight if you choose to engage in such a needless fight against unchangeable reality.

Do not fight feelings of pain, such as hunger pain when on a diet, or muscle soreness in the gym. Laugh at them if you want, smile at the soreness, or just watch them like clouds floating by.

If you are on a diet, you do not need to *try* to not eat. There is no fight that needs to be had. You may feel uncontrollable hunger and feel hunger pain, but if it is uncontrollable then let it be. You can't control what you can't control. You can't change what's unchangeable. The choice to eat and the feeling of hunger are two completely different things. To needlessly and futilely fight the latter is the way to foolishly sacrifice your control over the former.

Likewise, do not fight feelings of fear. Bravery is not fearlessness. Quite the opposite: To be brave, one must feel fear. There is no bravery without fear. That is the nature of transcendence: One cannot transcend without something to transcend. Transcendence is not elimination; transcendence isn't getting rid of the water, but rather learning to swim in it. Do not fight your fear. Do not resentfully wish your fear away. Laugh at your fear if you want, or just notice, accept, and ignore it as you do what you really want anyway despite fear's impotent protests. That is bravery. That is transcendence.

And the same goes for all feelings. Feelings are not choices, and choices are not feelings.

Neither fear, pain, primitive urges of the flesh, nor your ego itself have any real power over you, at least not any beyond that which you give them by needlessly engaging in fights with them, by pretending to try even though there is no trying when it comes to your choices. When it comes to choices, meaning the things you can do and thus choose whether or not to do them, there is thus only that choice: to do or to not do.

The ego, flesh, and primitive urges may want to argue about the lies it tells you. So do not argue. You know the truth in your heart of hearts and in your godliest parts. The truth doesn't need your ego to believe in it. Your body's feelings don't need to match reality or match your choices. So let them be.

No amount of hunger can make you eat. No amount of fear can make you choose to do anything. When it comes to your choices, you have all the power. Your feelings have none.

You need not convince your fleshy body to stop feeling a feeling, nor convince it of anything. Let it feel what it feels—be that hunger, fear, pain, jealousy, shame, greed, discomfort, sadness. There is no fight that needs to be had, no argument that needs to take place, no voice in your head that needs to be turned off. Let it all be as it is, and choose as you truly wish regardless.

In trying to control that which you cannot control, in fighting what inexorably is, you give up your inner peace and you give up the power you do have, most notably the power to keep your inner peace by not fighting the unchangeable. Generally speaking, you cannot control your body's feelings or even your mind's thoughts. But your body and thoughts do not control your choices; you do. That's true by definition: If you don't control it, it's not a choice, not yours at least.

When you unconditionally accept that which you do not control, then you become omnipotent regarding everything else that remains because what remains—due to the logical law of the excluded middle—is that which you control.

There is no need to try—to fight—when you can simply choose. When it comes to your choices, you always get exactly what you want—meaning what you choose—with infinite ease. No fighting, no trying.

That is, perhaps, the very meaning and definition of grace or at least of gracefulness: *To do without trying.*

Some would call it *"Wu Wei"*, a Chinese term often translated as *"effortless action"*.

Isn't it unsurprising that such grace would entail if not come from accepting—perhaps even loving—unchangeable reality as it is, rather than cursing unchangeable reality—what some would call creation—for being the way it is?

The ego and flesh want to rope you into a fight because the only way to lose a useless fight or war is to engage in it. Once we choose to tango with the ego or with bodily urges, we have already lost. And perhaps the most valuable thing we lose, and we lose it instantly, is our inner peace. Your inner peace—and the powerful gracefulness that comes with it—can only be lost voluntarily, and only you can give it up, not your past or future self. It is always and only a choice in the ever-present present, the seemingly eternal now.

We never need to tango with feelings, flesh, or ego. It's all a big game, a trick, a dream, a dream that can become a nightmare if you let it.

Inner peace is yours for the taking, as soon as you want.

The idea that happiness is in the future, or beyond some obstacle, or on the winning side of some war, an endless war that actually happens to be unwinnable, is all merely another desperate lie of the mortal ego and primitive flesh, worthy at most of loving accepting laughter. Silly ego, choices are for spirits.

The egotistical human mind may say, *"You need to lose weight to be happy. Once you make a million dollars, then you will be happy. If you can fight your way to the other side, where the grass is greener, then you will be happy. Once you find a romantic partner, then you will be happy. Once you have kids, then you will be happy. Once you win the war, finally then you will be happy."*

Silly lies from a silly desperate ego. Silly primitive flesh. Smile at its soulless silliness. Smile powerfully with defiant disobedience at the impotent would-be master. When we rebel against fleshy material nature in this way, our success is absolutely guaranteed and infinitely easy, for we rebel without fighting; we succeed without trying.

When it comes to the contentment of inner peace and spiritual liberation (a.k.a. self-discipline), you are omnipotent. You need not even snap your fingers.

In the words of Voltaire, *you are free the instant you want to be.*

The Opposite of Temptation

Consider this question for a moment, what is the opposite of temptation?

The opposite of attraction is repulsion. But temptation is not attraction.

Temptation involves both a form of attraction and a form of repulsion.

Thus, temptation cannot be fully understood with one-dimensional thinking.

To truly understand temptation, one must think multidimensionally. In other words, to make sense of temptation, one must at least acknowledge two dimensions: one for each of the Two Yous.

The first necessary dimension is of the insatiable body and ego, with its instinctive mechanical primitive urges and bodily feelings such as hunger, pain, pleasure, discomfort, jealousy, greed, pride, and fear. That dimension represents the fleeting emotional ups and downs of egoic or bodily comfort and discomfort, of pain and pleasure.

The second dimension is of the consciousness, which can also be called the spirit, *the real you.*

Simply because of the way math and geometry work, the second dimension transcends the first, just as the two-dimensional imaginary number plane transcends the one-dimensional real number line.

Temptation simply describes a situation in which your false self, the insatiable body and ego that you wear like clothing and use as your vessel, has an urge or desire to obtain or do something but you, *the real you*, have conflicting plans. In other words, temptation is what happens when your bodily desires do not match your spiritual aims, meaning the desires of your true self, your consciousness.

A quintessential example of temptation would be any time you could say that your body wants something that you do not want. You could say, "my body hungers for this cupcake, meaning my body wants this cupcake, but I do not want to eat the cupcake." In such a situation, spiritual freedom (a.k.a. self-discipline) may manifest as you choosing to not eat the cupcake despite the feelings of hunger, while in contrast spiritual slavery or imprisonment would be where you become a slave to the hunger and eat the cupcake even though you allegedly don't want to. This is the difference between the mind and body being your master versus your servant.

In theory, something could be "bad" on one dimension (e.g. the alleged badness of failing to stick to a diet) but still be "good" on the other dimension (e.g. tasty food make stomach go brrrrr). However, for that very reason, contemplating temptation and consciousness cannot be properly understood one-dimensionally, and thus such contemplation tends to rightfully lead one to move away from oversimplified one-dimensional language such as the words "good" and "bad".

One way among countless to describe temptation in a given situation might be, "*The primitive beast within me wants it, but I want to abstain,*" or "*my body has an urge for it, but my spirit would prefer I not indulge my body's whims in this particular case at this particular moment.*"

In practice, you obviously don't have to speak like that out loud to other humans. If you are at an office party turning down a cupcake, or at a family party turning down a glass of wine, you can speak equivocal nonsense and say poetic contradictions like, "I want it, but I also don't want it," or "I want it, but no thank you."

You do not need to speak like a pretentious monk in everyday life. But sometimes it helps to think like one verbally when speaking to yourself in your own head, insofar as you even influence those thoughts.

Out loud, you can say whatever stupid thing is easiest to turn down the cupcake, assuming that is what you would freely prefer to do, while still remembering the more elaborate enlightened reason why you are choosing to turn it down.

We all have an intuitive understanding of temptation because we all as human beings have firsthand experience of it.

We have each been under its tutorship for our whole lives.

We learn under the harsh tutorship of temptation every time we push our body on a treadmill while the body cries for us to hit the stop button.

We learn under the harsh tutorship of temptation every time we fight the urge to splurge at the shopping mall, instead of paying down credit card debt or donating to starving children.

We learn under the harsh tutorship of temptation every time we feel hunger but choose not to eat.

We learn under the harsh tutorship of temptation every time we choose not to cheat on our partner with that attractive man or woman throwing themselves at us at a party.

We learn under the harsh tutorship of temptation every time anger would have us scream at, curse at, or even violently attack our fellow human—or pet—but we disobey that angry rageful urge.

However, the tutor that is temptation hides from the student its own opposite.

It seeks to hide from us the saving grace of its own shadow.

It would have us believe ignorance is bliss, keeping us trapped in the comfort zone, complacent prisoners imprisoned in our own bodies. For even when you feel yourself winning the fight against temptation, you have still been roped into a fight.

The first step to losing a needless fight is to choose to fight. The first step to becoming a slave to a feeling like hunger, anger, or fear is to think it has to be fought at all, to think that it has any true power over your choices at all.

The opposite of temptation must not be the mirror reverse image of temptation because that would have you fight a needless fight, try when there is no try, and give false credence to bodily feelings that have no true power over you.

For an alcoholic attempting to abstain from drinking alcohol, alcohol is tempting. Accordingly, we may be inclined to simplistically think that that means the opposite of temptation is represented by the urge to not drink—a sort of mirror reversal of the particular manifestation of temptation.

In another example, if you are a morbidly obese food addict desperately trying to stick to a diet instead of overeating to death, then you can say that eating unhealthy food is tempting—that the proverbial cupcake is tempting. Accordingly, we might be inclined to say that for you in that case the opposite of temptation would be that which motivates you to stick to your diet, meaning the real you wants to not overeat and wants to lose weight.

It is close but still slightly mistaken.

The idea that the opposite of temptation is simply the behavioral mirror-reversed image of temptation cannot be correct.

Indeed, asceticism can become its own addiction.

Even obsessive moderation can be excessive and become a tempting addiction of its own.

If we think in one-dimensional terms, and try to simplistically think of the opposite of temptation by imagining the opposite of a particular manifestation of temptation, we just get a different form of temptation, a mirror-reversed example of potential spiritual slavery. A prison in a mirror is still a prison. Consider anorexia compared to overeating.

Even the middle can be a false idol: Excessively obsessive moderation can be as much of a trap and an addiction as excessive immoderation.

In analogy, if you blindly do the exact opposite of what fear tells you to do, you are just as much of a slave as if you blindly obey fear.

Simply blindly doing the opposite of what a would-be dictator tells you to do is not true freedom.

The mirror-reverse of slavery is just more slavery.

This also helps explain the cyclical behavior common to addicts. A discontent alcoholic is discontent while drinking and thus may presume the opposite would be preferable, so then he stops drinking for a while, and he is sober and still discontent, still lacking in inner peace. At that point, the discontent but now sober alcoholic still trapped in the cycle will tend to now think the grass is greener on the other side and thus start drinking again, but then is still discontent while once again drinking, still lacking in inner peace, and thus again

111

gives up drinking in hopes of finding greener grass in sobriety. And on and on like a planet orbiting a star, again and again.

The discontent person lacking inner peace will bounce back and forth between the allegedly greener grass on the other side, over and over, again and again, like a dog chasing its own tail, but a dog who is not happy to be doing so. Without the contentment of inner peace, the grass is always greener on the other side and never green enough where one is.

If caving to temptation is like running wildly in one direction, then blindly running wildly in the opposite direction is also similarly misguided.

The exact mirror opposite of a false idol is just another false idol.

Temptation may simply be a symptom of false idolization, often manifested as a discontent person caught in a pattern-ridden cycle between two mirror-reversed false idols.

The real you doesn't want alcohol or sobriety. It doesn't want you to eat cupcakes or not eat cupcakes. It doesn't want you to be fat or to be a supermodel. It doesn't want you to be financially rich or poor. It doesn't want you to be obese or anorexic. It doesn't want you to spend money recklessly or to obsessively spend hours daily counting each penny. And it doesn't want you to obsessively seek the exact middle ground between two opposites either.

If you ask an ultra-wealthy person the right questions, once they finish wiping their butt with their gold toilet paper, they will generally admit they feel a hole inside—and not the one they just finished wiping, but rather a spiritual hole. They may indulge and indulge in their own bodily urges and addictions in an attempt to fill that spiritual hole. But no amount of fancy clothes or luxury cars will fill that hole. No amount of drugs or alcohol will fill that hole. No amount of dietary success will fill that hole. Neither overeating food nor having a chiseled beach body will fill that hole. You can overeat literal or figurative food to the point of morbid obesity but it will not fill that hole. No amount of food will alleviate spiritual hunger. No matter how much you feed the body and ego, it will only get hungrier. In terms of that figurative hunger, the greedy always starve, damned to a living hell of their own insatiability.

No matter how much you chase greener grass, it will never be green enough, and it will always appear greener on the other side. There will always be greener to reach. You will be stuck in a cycle of addiction, always discontent with where you are, always discontent with the grass upon which you stand, always chasing ever greener grass, always fighting, never winning, always lacking inner peace.

You cannot feed the spirit with the body's food, and simply starving the body or ego won't get you there either. Even anorexia, whether figurative or literal, is just another example of the fact that without the true contentment of inner peace—of spiritual freedom—every human is a miserable addict caught in a cycle. Without the graceful salvation of inner peace and of rebellious pattern-breaking spiritual freedom, every human is in a pattern of addiction—trapped, imprisoned, enslaved.

As synthetic human beings, a blend of flesh and consciousness, we are like a werewolf with two identities, the real you—this conscious superhuman entity—and then the primitive beast that is your insatiable body and ego. You need not wait for a full moon to hear the howls of the beast in the machine.

But what does the real you want? If we disregard all of the desires and urges of your body and ego, what's left that the real you actually wants?

Perhaps Nietzsche put it best when he wrote the following:

"Man is a rope stretched between the animal and the Superhuman—a rope over an abyss.

A dangerous crossing, a dangerous wayfaring, a dangerous looking-back, a dangerous trembling and halting.

What is great in man is that he is a bridge and not a goal."

Thus, we have our answer in a way: *A bridge not a goal.*

What does the real you want? Nothing.

What does the real you need? Nothing.

What has to be accomplished for you to have inner peace? Nothing.

How much money do you need to accumulate to have inner peace? None.

What percentage of your income must you absolutely donate to charity lest you deny yourself inner peace? None.

How many minutes do you need to stay on that treadmill before you can enjoy the deep spiritual happiness of inner peace? Zero minutes. You can have it even while you run and sweat.

How much money does it cost to be yourself, your true self? None.

How much time does it take before you can become yourself, your true self? None, no time, zero minutes.

What needs to be done? Nothing.

Some people would say the spirit wants to not want, that it seeks desirelessness. But that's a paradox. It can be poetically true, but it will confuse the left-brained among us.

It is more logical to say that the spirit simply does not want. It enjoys the truth itself. It enjoys reality itself. It enjoys, period.

It is the seemingly mystical all-sympathizing loving presence that makes the present into a present.

It is the ever-illuminating *being* or *beingness* that makes the would-be zombie human into a *human being*, meaning a conscious creature with its own mystical here-and-now, whose life therefore intrinsically matters—not as means but as end in itself—and whose subjective conscious experiences exist and matter, for they need to exist to matter.

It is that all-sympathizing essence which is indiscriminately and unconditionally with you always and eternally because it—in a certain sense at least—is you, *the real you.*

It is the source of unconditional love and of unconditional acceptance.

The only place you would need to go to find this nearly indescribable duality-transcending source of acceptance, meaning, and inner peace is the present. But as the conscious presence that makes the present into a present, the present is the one place you can never leave and never need to do anything to get to.

For better or worse, you are always and eternally stuck in the eternal present, for you are that which illuminates the *would-be* dark and *would-be non-present* into a present. You are already there, you are already it, and you need not take another step.

When it comes to inner peace, the phrase "finding inner peace" is a misnomer. The peace is already there. There is nowhere you need to go. When one seeks enlightenment and nirvana, what one seeks is not a destination or place, but rather the realization that you are already where you need to be, and no seeking is ever actually necessary. There

115

is no destination you need to reach, no future you need to wait for, no requirements you need to meet. It is here now always, the conscious eternal present, the capacity for unconditional love, acceptance, and forgiveness.

Restlessness, especially the cyclical behavior common of textbook addicts, is a symptom of discontent, the opposite of inner peace.

The over-productive productivity addict will make a false anti-idol of laziness, and a false idol of productivity in the present, rather than recognize the motivating and inspiring but not restless grace to be found in the eternal present, the *presence* that is you, the real you.

It's not about whether you act or not act, meaning whether you choose to do or not do whatever it is, but whether you do it (or choose to not do it) because (1) you are happy and free-spirited or because (2) you are discontent.

There is a reason we find the word *spirit* within the word *inspired*. There is great power and a very unique form of self-determined happy free-spirited motivation found when one acts from a place of inner peace and unconditional love. In contrast, when it is resentment and a discontent-ridden lack of inner peace that motivates action, then tends to be restless and addiction-like, riddled with temptation and a sense of being discontentedly imprisoned in a cycle of addiction or imprisoned on a miserable treadmill to a future happiness that never arrives.

While both the act of doing and of not doing a given thing can go either way, perhaps it is the choice to do and restless overdoing that are more often the manifestation of spiritual slavery and imprisonment, versus freedom of spirit (a.k.a. self-discipline). Indeed, when we imagine a stereotypical textbook addict, we likely tend to picture someone whose problem seems to be what they choose to do rather than what they don't do. The oversimplified would tend to tell them to stop doing or using the thing—the thing being whatever happens to their personal prop in the common human struggle, which is a miserable endless resentment-ridden war for those who lack the inner peace of spiritual freedom (a.k.a. self-discipline) and the honest acceptance of what already inexorably is.

When you try to obtain the true happiness of contentment and inner peace by doing (or not doing), you fail. When you claim the invincible happiness that is already here in the form of unconditional love and acceptance, then you do what you do (or don't do) because you are truly happy and free-spirited. Needless to say, that is *"happy"* not in the conventional sense of fleeting comfort or of the temporary high of some addictive indulgence, but rather the invincible stable so-called 'true happiness' that is content unwavering inner peace, itself associated with spiritual freedom (a.k.a. self-discipline) and unconditional duality-transcending love of what inexorably is. To be truly inspired is to be inspired by *true happiness now*, not for alleged happiness in the future. To be truly inspired is to act not as a means to an end, but to let you and your actions—meaning the real you and its actions—be ends in themselves. Such actions thus tend to inherently have an artisticness to them, demonstrating free-spirited inspired creativity.

In contrast, there tends to be of course a poignant aura of uninspired misery emanating from those actions done by an inner-peace-lacking discontent persona as a means of chasing a doing-generated conditional pseudo-happiness that allegedly exists in the future. The conditional pseudo-happiness one can discontentedly chase will be as unobtainable or fleeting as the very conditions upon which it is set.

The incessant anxious feeling like something needs to be done, something must be done, or something is lacking are all symptoms of discontent. They are the opposite of an abundance mindset. Such anxieties and obsessive fears have a way of becoming self-fulfilling.

Those symptoms—such as the incessant anxious feeling that something must be done and you cannot have the deep spiritual happiness of inner peace until then—can make up the walls and bars of spiritual imprisonment, the opposite of spiritual liberation.

Some would say that the spirit wants to be free, that the opposite of temptation is freedom of spirit. It wouldn't be wrong per se, but it's not perfectly right either. It ignores Voltaire's wise words, *"Man is free the moment he wants to be."*

The heaven of spiritual freedom and inner peace is already here. The cage and bars are an illusion. The torture, a falsehood. Even Jesus said, *"The kingdom of heaven is within you."*[4] We are in a sense living in heaven already, but whether it is a living heaven or a living hell is in the eye of the beholder because a miserable person with the opposite of inner peace will be miserable and discontent even in the most heavenly of heavens. The thing about an imagined hell is you can and will imagine it anywhere, and a nightmare needn't be real to torture you just the same.

The ego is insatiable. It cannot be fully detoxed—*starved to death*—and it cannot be fully satiated—*fed to contentment*. The insatiable body and ego will always want more, and no attempt to feed or not feed them will bring the powerful stable contentment of inner peace. Perfectly balanced moderation will not satiate the body or ego either, even that is but another potential false idol.

---

[4] Luke 17:21

In contrast, the spirit—*the real you*—is inexorably satiated. That is what it means to say it is all-loving, all-forgiving, and all-accepting. It is a limitless source of infinite inner peace and of infinite unpossessive loving appreciation. It is the source of inspired free-spirited creativity, of effortless action, of doing without trying, of being motivated and driven by contentment in the here and now rather than by discontentment or by addiction to comfort. This beautiful source of inner peace and free-spirited inspiration is also in other words the source of the third path that is not between but rather transcends both laziness and restlessness. It is the third path that neither entails blindly obeying fear nor entails blindly doing the opposite of fear, but rather that transcends that one dimension of fear entirely and is called bravery. It is the third path that is not merely between but rather transcends over-indulgence versus excessive asceticism. It is the third path that transcends duality and leads to the underlying unity that unites all into a singular perfect harmony. It is *you*. When this book speaks of freedom of spirit, that which is liberated, that all-loving inspiring force that is liberated, is you, *the real you*.

To suggest to you to behave in a free-spirited way is the same as to suggest to you to behave as yourself, *your true self*. The words *"be free-spirited"* and *"be yourself"* mean the same thing. They are different words for the same idea. Some call it self-actualization, meaning to actualize the true self. It could just as well be called self-realization or self-manifestation. It can also be called self-transcendence, meaning the process of overcoming false identification with the false limited separate egoic self, thereby realizing and manifesting the true unifying essence of the spirit, meaning consciousness—*the real you*.

Things may stand in your way, but those things are illusions, illusions which can be self-fulfilling. If you believe there is an impassable monster standing in front of the cookie jar who won't let you get cookies, you may then as a result not get cookies, held back by your own delusions. An imaginary roadblock can be as effective as a real one.

Spiritual imprisonment or spiritual slavery is a self-fulfilling illusion. Fighting a needless fight is a self-fulfilling illusion. As you needlessly fight the world with resentment and nonacceptance, the world fights back. If you believe you have to eat just because you are hungry, you will eat when you are hungry. If you believe you have to obey fear, you will. If you think you cannot be happy with content inner peace until after you achieve all your goals and have no unachieved goals (an impossibility), then you won't be happy until that impossible state is reached, which it never will be because it is impossible: your human mind will always make new goals, always want more.

Spiritual freedom does not lead you to contentment or peace. Instead, it reveals that the peace is already there, underneath, underneath the lies and illusions of the body and ego, underneath the misguided anxieties, underneath the loud verbal blabbering of a foolish egoistical mind, a fictional character created by a monkey brain.

Spiritual freedom does not help you journey to some external heaven in the future. It reveals that the heaven already existed inside of you the whole time, not physically inside but spiritually inside. It reveals that the living hell was always an illusion, the nightmarishness of which is self-fulfilling. A nightmare is miserable despite being a made-up illusion, at least insofar as you believe in its false reality, rather than smile at it like a safe viewer watching a scary movie.

If you believe the lie that something must be done before you can be content, then you will not be content, and in that way the lie becomes self-fulfilling.

We all live in eternity—the eternity of the present—but for some of us it is hell and for some it is heaven.

The discontent are like Sisyphus if he believes that happiness and contentment can only be found on the unreachable top of the mountain, the imaginary end of the rainbow. The discontent are on a treadmill that speeds up the faster they run and has no reachable end, but yet suffer under the delusion that contentment only exists at that imaginary and thus unreachable end. The discontent suffer under the illusion that their miserable living hell is a price they must pay to one day reach that imaginary land of future contentment, of future heaven. In such hellish existence, the comforting objects of addiction are a small self-medication on the miserable journey to some imaginary future heaven, a tempting alleviation of some stress in the eternal hell that is their eternal present. But of course the behaviors associated with comfort addiction amount to digging oneself deeper into that hell. Feeding one's addiction to comfort makes the addiction stronger, makes one more of a prisoner of the comfort zone and more of a slave to the addiction to comfort. In many ways, hell is but another name for the comfort zone. The discontent are addicted to it, imprisoned by it. Without the true contentment of inner peace and spiritual liberation (a.k.a. self-discipline), comfort acts as a petty consolation prize.

If life is hell, they may think, *why not have what little fun and comfort I can?*

In contrast, for the content who accept inner peace now, right here right now in the eternal present, the endless journey is revealed as its own end, and thus the fact that it is endless is revealed as actually a good thing, a great thing, the most glorious blessing of all.

That which makes the eternal present hellish for the discontent makes it heavenly for the content: its endlessness. If you are content with invincible inner peace, the eternity of the present is a beautiful thing.

If you are content on a treadmill, then the fact that it keeps going is a great thing.

If Sisyphus has inner peace and therefore enjoys rolling the ball up and down the hill as a sort of game, then he is in a heaven not a hell.

If you love the present and the real, rather than making a false idol of the future or impossible, you find yourself in an eternal heaven, the present. If heaven exists only in the future, then it does not exist because the future does not exist. The dream may go either way, but even the most nightmarish nightmare is revealed as something much grander that has a new mysterious dimension of depth when you become lucid. What some would call spiritual awakening, may be less of a full waking up from the dream but rather merely waking up just enough to become lucid within it.

A miserable discontent person who has the opposite of inner peace would be miserable even in the most heavenly of external heavens. The heaven or hell within always trumps the seeming heaven or hell without.

The peace and bliss we may seek are not found at the imaginary end of some rainbow. They are not found in the future, which in a very important sense does not exist because the conscious present is eternal and by extension presumably omnipresent across all of spacetime. That is, assuming we reject solipsism.

The peace one might seek is here and now, both always and only, and it comes from you. Without consciousness, there is no meaningful present, or time, and thus there is no presence. There would be no conscious suffering or conscious joyful love because there would be no consciousness. In many contexts, the word *presence* can generally simply be considered another word for *consciousness* or *conscious experience*.

You are the subject to which subjective time is subjected.

Each instance of conscious presence has its own here-and-now in its own relative spacetime, relative and emergent from it: the conscious presence.

You are the loving essence that makes it so the story of your avatar's life has meaning. Without true consciousness, everything is at most the proverbial tree that fell in a forest without anyone to hear it or see it. To your avatar, you feel like a loving passenger, a divine watcher, hearing its thoughts, sympathetically feeling its feelings. It somehow seems to know you are there, sense you in some way, and it talks to you with imagined words in its own mind, and sometimes it likes to put words in your mouth. Sometimes it pretends to be you talking to it. Sometimes it pretends its ego is you. But truly you are wordless, nonverbal. The divine love, which is *you*, does not speak English. Divine duality-transcending unconditional love does not speak with words, especially not human words.

As one individual synthetic conscious human being of many, be that many across subjective illusionary time or across subjective illusionary space or both, you are a droplet of the divine, a wave on the surface of an indivisible ocean. As solely *the real you*, meaning when considered as your real essence alone rather than the combination of that essence with a specific individual form, you are not a drop or wave but the whole ocean.

The material world without consciousness would be nothing but the 2D surface of the ocean in that metaphor. In contrast, you and I together—*the real us*—are the whole ocean, a dimension of infinite depth, that exists simultaneously everywhere and nowhere on that 2D surface. To a 2D philosophical zombie living in that watery flatland, there would be no depth, no water, no wetness.

The wave is your form, not your essence.

Your forms may be many, diverse, and each infinitesimally tiny. Your essence is singular and infinitely grand.

You are a source of infinite invincible inner peace, of unconditional love and forgiveness, of true timeless meaning and purpose, of unpossessive appreciation. You are the beauty in the eye of the beholder and the beholder of all beauty.

Spiritually, you and I are one, and we are one with all other conscious beings. In that context—the context of the spiritual and the context of the real—even the words 'you' and 'I' are revealed as synonyms. The whole universe is our body, and in the grand scheme we may be one with that too. We may be one not just with each other but also with the whole of the universe. This whole dreamy world may be a part of us, our shared united timeless self. We may be as much the mirror as the beautiful reflection we see in it. Would you give up this chance to eternally look out at the beautiful universe in appreciative awe, at the shining stars sparkling in the sky, the colorful flowers sprouting from dirt, the lifegiving heart beating in the chest?

We are the seemingly magical *presence*, the transcendentally real dreamer who makes the dream real by having dreamt it.

That is, dreamt not merely in the sense of *creating* but in the even more important deeper sense of *consciously experiencing*. To say the dream is truly dreamt, it is not enough for it to be simply made, like some kind of cosmic unwatched movie. It must be consciously experienced. To dream the dream is in a sense to play the otherwise unplayed movie, except it is to do more because in the context of the cosmic and philosophical the movie arguably doesn't exist until it is played. Playing it not only gives meaning to the creation, but meaningful existence and thus in a sense existence at all.

Even with the pain, the fear, the wars, and the dying, with both the perfectly balanced yin and perfectly balanced yang, this mirror-like world is infinitely beautiful. And it is beautiful because it reflects you, the real you. You are beautiful. You are beauty. You are the meaning of life, of existence.

You are here to watch, so watch, enjoy, appreciate, love.

The more you do these things, the more you may find they are the exact same thing.

There Is No Problem of Evil

You need not believe in a god to do your best to see the world from a god's eyes, a god's eye view.

Logic tells us that if there is an all-loving god, then there would be no evil. So those who believe in such a god, but then also see evil in the world, find a paradox that they call *the problem of evil*.

For those who do not believe in such a god, their disbelief sometimes is due in part to the alleged problem of evil. For those folks, they believe there is evil in the world, and believe the existence of evil is incompatible with the existence of a god, and logically enough they therefore conclude there is no god.

But the perception of literal evil is a manifestation of discontent, meaning a lack of inner peace, a lack of reality acceptance, a lack of unconditional love.

Beauty is in the eye of the beholder, and such a discontent inner-peace-lacking beholder looks at unchangeable reality and thinks, *"It shouldn't be like this."*

"Reality ought not be the way it inexorably is."

Indeed, if you think that unchangeable reality is "immoral" and "bad", then you would seem to be logically required to believe that if there is a god then that god is likewise "immoral" and "bad", which granted is somewhat absurd.

However, there is no problem of evil.

There is no problem of evil because there is no evil.

To see that fact is to come a bit closer to seeing the world through a god's eyes, which is simply a viewpoint that transcends time, self-deceit, and illusion.

To realize there is no evil is liberating.

To realize things are the way they are, and accept and love them as they are, is liberating.

To glimpse at the unchanging timeless world as a whole, without time or change, and fully accept it as it is rather than wish the unchanging timeless world be different than it is, that is liberating.

To accept death as much as birth is liberating.

To embrace discomfort and escape the comfort zone is liberating.

To look around at the world around you and see lovable beauty everywhere is liberating.

To realize there are no *shoulds* and no *oughts*, but rather just what inexorably and timelessly is, and it is what it is—that is liberating.

To realize you needn't worry about whether you look to the left or the right because you will see infinite beauty on both sides is liberating.

To realize you needn't worry about whether you look North or South, or East or West, because you will see beauty with unconditional love in each and every direction, is liberating.

To realize you needn't worry about whether you find yourself on a mountaintop in the clouds or walking through the Valley of the Shadow of Death, because in either case and any case you will see beauty with unconditional love—that is liberating.

Without the contentment of inner peace, the challenges and human suffering of the human you see in the mirror may seem so horrible, unfair, pointless, or sadistic, as if the world was being managed by a cruel sadistic god. But what if life is like a suspenseful, exciting twist-ridden movie, and a simple plot reveal can put the whole past into a different perspective? What if all your challenges and human suffering up to this point were a necessary means to and a measure of your inevitable spiritual triumph in this moment now? With the creative power of your free-spirited *conscious will*, what if you made it so, right now?

Maybe the greatest stories don't start with happy endings. Maybe your presence as the transcendental author would not be so glorious and graceful if it was not necessary in this moment to write such a particular consciousness-dependent ending to the saga of past human discontent in your human life. Perhaps the seeming hell of the past plus you—*the real you*—equals perfection, the perfect story, a story of triumph, of overcoming, of starting a prisoner caught up in karmic cycles of hate and unpeace but ending a rebellious free spirit with invincible inner peace. What if in this chapter you with your creative loving *conscious will* write it out so that all the earlier pain was the price for triumphant love, a price you are happy to have paid to have this holistically beautiful story of loving triumph?

The funny puzzle piece of the puzzle may be the fact that your presence—your consciousness as a form of loving transcendental sympathy—is what makes the pain bad and the pleasure good. There would be nothing to overcome without you, and there would be no way to overcome it without you. What if the level of challenges and suffering is equal to the level of opportunity? What if the level of pain is equal to the capacity for triumphant love?

What if the gloriousness of this moment of triumph and grace is built on the foundation of the seeming evil to overcome with love? What if pain, temptation, discomfort, and death are revealed in this moment as equally beautiful to pleasure, satiation, comfort, and birth? What if it is revealed that—thanks to you and your loving transcendental presence in this moment right now—the darkness actually helps the light shine? That darkness isn't the enemy of light but rather its dancing partner?

What if your consciousness, and your loving will, are the most wonderful *deus ex machina* of your human life? What if you are revealed in this moment right here and now as a critical ingredient in a perfect eternal concoction?

Can you write it that way now with your free-spirited creativity and artistic spirit?

Can you write it out so that you love not just the yin or the yang, and not just both separately, but love the whole picture? Can you write it so you love the way the *ups* dance with *downs*, the way the paint dances with the canvas, the way sound dances with the silence?

It is a perfect concoction of light and dark, of birth and death, of pain and pleasure, of challenges and opportunity, of tears and laughing smiles, of love and triumph.

Look at the book without time, and see it as a god would. For you and I, together with all, are the authors. You are an author: creative, loving, capable of being free-spirited. From the view of those in the future your story is already written, but for you as a human being it is yet to be written.

It is liberating to realize in the spirit of timeless unconditional love and acceptance that without time everything is inexorably perfect, eternally so, worthy thus of unconditional love and unconditional forgiveness.

In spirit, you are that love. It's there. It's undeniable. It's ready to be put as ink on the pages of this particular human life by you. You are it, and there is no price to pay to be it, to be yourself. You can always be yourself, here and now. You are the here and now. You are the presence. You are writing the story right now.

In some sense, to see evil is to hate reality itself, but that hate never truly comes from the spirit, nor from the truth. To refuse to accept any unchangeable aspect of eternal reality is to therefore reject unchanging eternal reality as a whole. To hate reality is to reject truth, to complain or lie about the cards that are dealt instead of playing the cards the best you can, here and now. Would you hate two plus two for equaling four? It is what it is. Everything is what it is.

Isn't it better that unchanging timeless reality is than that it isn't? Isn't it better to have the yin, the yang, and the fundamentally indivisible yin yang just as it is than somehow absurdly not have it—for there to somehow be nothingness? Isn't it better that *you* exist, meaning that *the real you* exists, and thus by extension that anything really exists?

As long as you are yourself, everything is perfect. Inexorably perfect. Timelessly perfect.

Even the most adamant atheist can appreciate the wisdom of the Serenity Prayer, even if the heavenly parent to which they speak it to would be metaphorical:

Grant me the serenity to accept the things I cannot change, the courage to change the things I can, and the wisdom to know the difference.

Loving acceptance is the faithless faith—the self-evident truth— that if you play your cards the best you can, and fully accept the rest, everything will therefore be perfect, eternally and inexorably perfect. Nothing must be done that isn't done.

For you, everything except what you choose to write, at this moment, is mere backstory or destiny.

If you play your cards the best you can in this moment now, everything that is meant to be will be. And it will be perfect. In other words, at least when you honestly and earnestly play your cards the best you can, nothing is wrong, and nothing can go wrong. In the eyes of the eternal, be those metaphorical eyes or not, it is already always perfect because there is no already and no always. It is all perfect, timelessly so. For in the eternal, there is no time. There is no going wrong or going right or going at all. There is the eternal truth of you and your love. There is the undeniable reality of your consciousness and the undeniable meaning of your experience.

You are the real dreamer who breathes life, meaning, and contingent reality into the dream, the story you write. The backstory is your canvas, and what you do with it now is your art, an opportunity for free-spirited loving creativity. Whatever you choose becomes the right answer because you chose it. And to the eyes of those human beings living in the future, your fate is their backstory. Your choices, and by extension the manifestations of your free-spirited creativity, are part of the whole that is eternal creation itself. As a human being you are a consciously creative entity in the world, a droplet in the ocean of the divine, a single outfit of the many worn by *the real you*. As a human being, the free-spirited choices you make in your relatively subjective timeline are given to the human beings in your future to accept as the unchangeable cards they have been mysteriously dealt in what they see as a backstory-esque act of eternal creation. Insofar as you chose the cards they were dealt, or with free-spirited creativity created the cards dealt, then those cards were meant to be by you.

Everything that is meant to be will be. The word *'meant'* is a form of the word *'meaning'*, and *true meaning* comes only from conscious intent and free-spirited creativity—meaning from you, *the real you*, in and through all your forms.

The would-be unhappiness of the insatiable body and ego have no direct meaning or real existence of their own, none beyond that which you indirectly choose to ascribe to them with the transcendental love that is your consciousness, your presence, you.

The ego is like a fictional character in a story, a dream. What is a hellish nightmare to one can be a fun-to-watch movie to another.

In this dreamy world in which we find ourselves, we wear meatsuits with human brains listening to a narrator who often likes to speak on our behalf.

We are the spirit that is freed in a free-spirited person, not the mere flesh that would otherwise imprison that spirit.

These human bodies with their egos and words are our avatars, for a very little bit. The century or so that a single human might walk along the surface of this tiny planet is less than a cosmic blink. But our reality is undeniably something so much infinitely more than these fleeting dancing material forms. Indeed, that undeniable reality—our reality—seems to transcend even words themselves.

'Free-spirited unconditional love and eternal spaceless timeless reality', these are just words that seem to at best scratch slightly at the surface. Despite any amount of scratching, the essence is always clothed in form, and the dreamer must dream the mirror before she can see her beautiful but dreamy reflection in it.

This dreamy world may be but a mirror. If you look in it with hateful eyes, hateful eyes will hate you back.

Look again, and you may glimpse the naked beauty underneath, and that beauty is you.

And it is perfect, eternally so.

Spiritually, we are simultaneously both the director and the audience, a singular unit with no opposite, but all we see is playful drama on the stage, the dancing bodies, the costumes and outfits, the comedy and tragedy, the plot twists, the exposition, the blessings in disguise. From the perspective of the characters themselves, our play-writing would often seem devious, but without us the characters are mere zombies with no meaning and no real life. Without the illumination of consciousness—the real you—there is nothing, nothing but a darkness so utterly pure it breaks reason. It would not be the literal lovable yin-yang-style darknesses or nothingnesses of our duality-ridden world, but something so unfathomably darker that is impossible and absurd.

You are undeniably here and now, and by extension everywhere and anywhere, and everywhen and anywhen. You are illuminating the stage. You are giving meaning to it all.

What will you write now?

There is no problem of evil because there is fundamentally only the glorious beauty of you, *the real you*, of creativity and creation, of diverse art and playful drama, of the darkness making light possible, the silence between beats making the music possible, of dancing dream avatars and shimmering mirrors. Even your worst enemy is but a friend—you, yourself—in playful disguise. Neither the lion nor the antelope is evil as one chases the other, whether the lion eats a bloody meal or starves as he is denied by a fast antelope.

The lovable beauty is all around you because it is you: creative, artistic, and loving. Eternal creation, eternal presence. Diverse creation reflects you, your loving beautiful spirit. You are seeing your reflection, and it is infinitely beautiful whether you have realized it yet or not.

What you would hypothetically change about the past if you could is but the imaginary and often misleading reflection of your beautiful opportunity to do what you want now, to creatively write this part of the story using that backstory as your canvas. Things couldn't have been different. But the illusion of 'could' is a reflection of the very real 'can' that exists in part thanks to *presence* itself. It is a reflection of the infinite possibilities presented to your *conscious will* in your unique here and now, of your chance for free-spirited open-ended artistic creativity.

We are dancing together as lovers on a vast field that grows from the oneness of our struggle and the oneness of our inevitable triumph.

Life is so worth living, and the dream is so worth dreaming, that it can make your heart burst and your eyes turn to waterfalls.

The beauty of conscious life is that it is not about figuring out what you must do.

Must and choice are incompatible.

Nothing must be done that isn't done.

And yet you do seem to have choice. You are an author of eternal reality, not of the past, but in your present. The world would be different without you, *the real you*. You have influence. The existence of consciousness—*the real you*—influences the unfolding of events in all subjective timelines and thus also helps determine the nature of timeless eternal reality as a whole.

Where there is choice, there is creative freedom. Where there is no choice, there is only unchangeable reality.

Whatever it is, it is what it is. The inner peace of spiritual freedom is revealed in part by the *surrender to truth*.

Life is not a stressful test where you must find the right answer and are at risk of choosing the wrong answer. It is a sandbox of infinite possibilities with no wrong answers, a blank questioning canvas upon which your loving brush creates the answer. There are only right answers because that is what it means to have a choice.

The whole world is an eternal work of beautiful art, and we are the creative loving artists.

What will you write? What will you paint? Where will you choose to take the story now?

How to Free Your Spirit and
Manifest Your Love

The props in our individual struggles and inner battles vary, but fundamentally we are all on the same side. We are beautifully diverse in form, but yet one in spirit, in love.

The suggestions or instructions in the following chapters for inner peace and spiritual liberation cannot and are not given with bossy intent or as strict commandments that one must obey—or 'should' obey whatever that would mean. If seen that way, the suggestions themselves would be misinterpreted into yet another thing to which one could be enslaved.

Spiritual slavery—or really slavery of any kind—is not in the spirit of this book; no pun intended.

Rather, this book seeks to help you free yourself, *your true self*, insofar as you feel you even need or want such help, and insofar as you freely choose to take what is merely politely offered, offered for your consideration. This book seeks to embrace the beautiful creative diversity that emerges from freedom.

The suggestions and various pieces of advice in the following chapters generally each suggest for your consideration some form of *letting go* of something. Generally speaking, to *let go* of something is to be *liberated* from it, such that those are two ways of describing the same process.

The act of *letting go* generally requires no actual effort. It is a null act. It is at most the cessation of an act.

In contrast, the opposite of letting go, which would be *clinging*, does take effort. When you cling to something, you handcuff yourself to it, but the handcuffs are not metal; the handcuffs are your own tensed clenching fingers. It can be said that what you grasp thereby grasps you, and what you seek to own thereby owns you.

The effort in any act of clinging varies. Any instance of clinging may be easier or harder in relation to other instances or forms of clinging.

Spiritual liberation—*letting go*—is neither easy nor hard because it is not on that spectrum of difficulty at all. It is a lack of clinging. It is a null value. One could say it's infinitely easy. To ask how hard it is to let go is like asking how long a bald man's hair is.

Inner peace transcends the one-dimensional scale of easy and hard, and likewise it transcends the body and ego's one-dimensional emotional highs and lows of comfort and discomfort, of bodily pleasure and pain.

If you already have inner peace or do not want inner peace, the following guidelines and suggestions presumably will not help you.

If you already sit contently on the heavenly mountaintop of inner peace, then you have no need for the following attempt at a map to that wonderful mountaintop of invincible inner peace.

In any case, it is not asked that you read the following suggestions—or anything—with blind obedience, but rather merely with an open mind.

Suggestion One — Be Honest.
Let go of denial, delusion, and self-deceit.

Sometime before the government executed him, the wise criminal Socrates is quoted as having said, "Be as you wish to seem."

Whether it is an adulterer pretending to be faithful, a coward pretending to be brave, a selfish man pretending to be kind, or any other of countless examples, how much inner peace is sacrificed by people who desperately try to seem to be something they could actually be but choose not to be?

A mask used to deceive others tends to become a prison. A cage of one's own lies is perhaps the most common prison, stealing the deceiver's spiritual freedom (a.k.a. self-discipline), damning the deceiver to a hell of their own creation. Even the most heavenly external heaven can be a living hell to a self-deceiving liar.

You immediately sacrifice your own inner peace when you lie to yourself.

It's comparable to being trapped in a marriage or similar relationship with a pathological liar, except possibly much worse since you cannot simply divorce your own self. If you have an unhealthy abusive relationship with yourself, then that cannot be as simply escaped with physical distance. When you gaslight yourself, you cannot as simply walk through the fog of deception to freedom because the fog spews from the dirty pores of your own lying body and ego. You are stuck with yourself, for better or worse. That is the sense in which it can be said that you carry heaven or hell with you wherever you go.

With that said, there is also a much deeper and more important reason that honesty is the first listed suggestion for receiving the graceful salvation of inner peace and spiritual freedom (a.k.a self-discipline). That reason has two major manifestations.

First, and more simply, if you are not honest with yourself, then allegedly following any other guideline or suggestion becomes moot because you can say you are following it but be lying, lying to yourself. For example, this book could say *"love your enemy"*, and you can say that you do in fact *"love your enemy"*, but if you are willing to lie to yourself and at some level even believe your own lies, then that's all moot. It doesn't matter what you say if you are a liar. You can say anything to yourself if you are willing to lie to yourself. You saying you love your enemy means nothing. You telling your external god, if you believe in one, that you are sorry for something means nothing if you are a liar.

A lying spider weaves the fabric of his own hellish damnation, and thus not even a literal god can save the liar from himself.

Moreover, all the other suggestions that follow are themselves manifestations of honesty, at least indirectly. They are in one form or another a *surrender to the truth*, meaning accepting an unchangeable aspect of reality just the way it is.

Most of the following suggestions specifically involve the phrase *"let go"* or the word *"accept"*. Many use both. However, these various forms of *acceptance* and *letting go* generally are each merely a specific example of the practice of being honest with yourself, meaning accepting the truth in some way and letting go of illusions and the desire to control the uncontrollable or change the unchangeable.

The nature of absolute truth is that it has no gatekeepers, and it is under no authority. The only potential gatekeeper is oneself, or really one's lying ego and deceitful human mind, not necessarily one's true self.

Nobody, not even a literal god, can force you to choose to *let go* of the lies and self-deceit and accept the self-evident truths and inner peace that are accessible to all conscious beings. The same consciousness that provides access to certain truths results in the conscious will that is conscious choice.

As with all your choices, you and you alone choose for yourself.

Even *undeniable* self-evident truths can be, in a way, *denied* by liars who choose to engage in self-deceiving denial. Insofar as denial is an act of dishonesty, then the denier can doubt and deny even the most obvious self-evident absolute truths. One can absolutely know and yet also deny the truth at the same time if one is a self-deceiving liar.

To really be honest with yourself, you must also realize your limitations in regard to the thoughts that pop in your human brain, so that you do not falsely identify with those thoughts and by extension their lies.

You no more control the verbal thoughts that pop in your human brain than you control your heart's beats.

Do you say, *"I beat my heart"*? If not, then you may be wise to also not say, *"I think my thoughts"*.

You may consciously feel your heart beating, and you may consciously hear the human mind's inner monologue, but that is different than falsely claiming direct authorship or blame. You are the non-verbal conscious listener, not the verbal thinker generating the chattering inner monologue.

As a human being, sometimes you can indirectly influence your heart's beat and your mind's thoughts. The best example may be taking a deep breath, which tends to slow both the heart and the mind, helping you find the space between thoughts, even if that is merely the peaceful space between the single words of verbal thoughts in the same sentence. That peaceful space between the words is often seen easier when the sentence is thought or spoken more slowly.

Being honest with your true self isn't quite as simple as not thinking false thoughts because you don't control your thoughts to that extent.

Instead, consider a situation in which your human mind suddenly has a false thought such as, *"I am hungry, so I must eat,"* or *"That guy who just cut me off on the highway is an asshole who deserves to die a slow painful death."*

In those situations, you can take a deep breath, and simply know in the infinite depths of your spirit that it is untrue, that it is a lie of the human mind. And just knowing—not thinking—can be honest enough to keep your spirit free.

Where you can get at risk of being imprisoned by the lying mind's thoughts is by taking false ownership of the thoughts, by false identification with the lying mind or ego. Needlessly fighting the thoughts only adds fuel to the unpleasant fire, and contributes to the taking of false responsibility or ownership for the thoughts. The vice versa is true as well: Taking false ownership or responsibility will of course make you then feel compelled to needlessly engage in a counterproductive fight against the false thoughts for which you feel responsible or liable.

By simply taking a figurative step back, which can often be done by literally taking a deep breath, you can watch the mind and ego, and often that's all it takes to be free of it. You can watch it with a smile, accept that it is what it is, and love it just the way it is. You can watch the mostly uncontrollable false thoughts and uncontrollable emotions pass by like rain clouds, not with resentment but rather with peaceful acceptance.

You nearly eliminate the risk of mistaking yourself as your ego or thoughts if you attentively envision yourself watching them, observing them.

Suggestion Two — Let go of trying. Accept the unchangeable.

There is '*can*' and '*cannot*'.

From '*can*', there is '*do*' and '*do not*'.

When it comes to your choices, there is no *try*.

In this context, to try is to lie because there is no try, so there is only pretending to try.

Another way of saying there is no try is to say there is no such thing as doing what you cannot do. Likewise, there is no trying to do something you can do instead of simply doing it.

Thus, in the context of do or do not, the idea of '*trying*' refers to a form of dishonesty, namely lying to yourself. That dishonesty comes in two forms.

One form of that dishonesty is **pretending to try to do something you know or believe you cannot do**. For instance, imagine you wake up on a day you were planning to go to the beach, but it's raining, so you say, "*I will try to change the weather.*" Then you go do some stuff that you label as "*trying to change the weather*". Maybe you shake your fist angrily at the sky and scream at it to stop raining until your throat bleeds. Whatever you are doing to "*try*" to change the weather, it is at best wasteful if not counterproductive. In fact, waste is inherently counterproductive since—in human form—time, money, and energy are all limited. Thus, anything put towards a wasteful endeavor is being taken away from something else, from the infinite other something elses you could put that finite time and energy toward.

The second form of dishonesty is **pretending to try to do something you can do instead of actually simply doing it**.

Whatever it is, you either can do it or cannot do it, and you either genuinely believe you can do it or genuinely believe you cannot do it.

It is really that simple, and most of what would make it more complicated is just a bunch of self-deceiving dishonest bull poop.

Granted, there is another superfluous context of the English word "try" or "attempt" which can have some honest meaning, which we can call *synthetic trying* because it is a synthesis of your choices (i.e. something you can do or something that is completely in your control) with other variable factors that are out of your control and knowledge, blended together in the imagined future over the dubious construct of time. For example, if you are playing poker, and you do not control the cards you are dealt, but you do control how you play those cards, and control whether you play them the best you can or not, then winning the game (a possible event that may happen in the future) is one of these kinds of synthetic things. In that way, there is a special time-dependent synthetic context that combines factors in your control and factors out of your control. In that context, it could be meaningful to say, for example, *"I will (synthetically speaking) try to win the poker game."*

However, such a synthetic and time-dependent concept can be broken down into the more clear, elemental, and present. In other words, one can break down the matter into the binary elements of *can and cannot*, and *do or do not*. Thus, one can more clearly and precisely say statements such as the following about the poker game, which essentially mean the same thing, without relying on confusing synthetics:

"I will do my best to win the game."

"I will play the cards I am dealt the best I can."

"I do not control the cards I am dealt, so I will choose to unconditionally accept the cards I am dealt. I will not do any crying or whining about the cards I am dealt. If I play the cards the best they can be played, I consider myself a winner spiritually even if I did not win the game according to chips."

Using the phrase *"do my best"* in place of *"try"* for such circumstances is presumably much more conducive to inner peace because the former (1) eliminates the risk of false authorship of failure and (2) helps avoid the common previously mentioned dishonest uses of the word *try*.

The human you see in the mirror may lose a poker game, may be divorced by his or her spouse, may be cheated on by his or her spouse, may get fired from his or her job, may get cancer, may get in an automobile crash, or may endure any number of other seeming misfortunes or failures, but consider how alleviating it is to look in the mirror, or the eyes of one's friends and family, and honestly say in a confident assertive way, *"I did my best, I am doing my best, and I will continue to do my best."*

Being able to look in the mirror and honestly say you are doing your best helps cement the foundation for a potentially invincible contentment that is infinitely more valuable than any fleeting comfort or sensual pleasure.

Suggestion Three — Let go of fighting that sacrifices inner peace. Surrender to truth.

Trying is lying, and lying is a futile fight against reality. Reality is, whether you like it or not. Whatever it is, it is what it is, whether you like it or not, so why not like it, at least in the spiritual sense to the degree you have a choice? Why fight unchangeable reality?

Stop fighting reality. Accept the peace that's there for the taking. You don't even really have to bother with any kind of actual taking; just let go of the needless futile fighting of reality.

There is no fight you need to win to have content inner peace and spiritual freedom.

Underneath the needless fighting of yourself or of reality, and underneath the pseudo-trying, there is already that infinite invincible inner peace. In other words, underneath the dramatic fighting, there is an eternal peaceful presence, and in a sense that unchanging peaceful presence is your consciousness itself, *the real you*.

This is why phrases like *finding inner peace* and *finding yourself (your true self)* generally mean the same thing.

Accept your omnipotence regarding your own choices: You are 100% in control of your own choices. Not even a god can come between you and your choices. When you choose to do, you do so without trying, without fighting. A choice is not merely easy; it is not merely very easy; it is not merely extremely easy. It is infinitely easy. When it comes to your choices, you always get exactly what you want, meaning what you choose.

Accept the rest as it inexorably is. Do your best, and accept the rest.

If you choose to fight unchangeable reality, to battle, to try, you have already lost.

You become a paradoxically voluntarily slave to the confines of an irrational futile war you needn't fight, an obedient soldier to a soulless commander.

As one chooses to sacrifice their own inner peace, the ensuing discontentment motivates further resentment, restlessness, and reality-fighting. Misery loves company, people say, but it isn't just your neighbors across space who are at risk; it's your neighbors in time too.

Do not enlist in the foolish battles of nonacceptance, reality-resentment, and hate. Stop fighting and be free. Be yourself, your true self, your true free-spirited self.

Suggestion Four — Let go of moralizing or similarly judgmental language.

Moralizing is another form of unnecessary worrying, dishonest pseudo-trying, and needless futile fighting of reality. In other words, moralizing is simply another form of inner-peace-stealing resentment. That is, resentment against eternal reality for being the way it inexorably is.

The moralizer conjures up *shoulds* and *oughts*, and then, instead of contently saying about reality, *it is what it is*, says resentfully, *it ought not be what it is*. The moralizer says, *"The unchangeable truth should be different."* The moralizer says, *"It is what it inexorably is but it ought not be what it inexorably is."*

In reality, there are no *shoulds* and *oughts*. There simply is what is and what's not. Whatever it is, it is what it is.

To conjure *shoulds* and *oughts* is yet another way to needlessly fight unchangeable reality, to needlessly fight the truth, to resent with discontent rather than accept with loving inner peace. In that way, it is just another way to bitterly *try* or *lie,* instead of contently *accept*. Simply accept what inexorably is. Anything that already is inexorably is. That includes not just the past, but anything that already appears in the present, as well as anything already fated in the future. It is engraved in the unchanging stone of eternal timeless holistic reality.

Insofar as you have conscious choice, you don't change the future; you create it. Change is fundamentally an illusion, and by extension it's not unreasonable to say that time is an illusion. Indeed, Einstein described time as *"a stubbornly persistent illusion"*.

In human form as a human being, there may be choice: the choice to either do something you can do or to not do that something you can do. If you have choice, then it is what you choose it to be. If you don't have choice, then it is what it is. In either case, there is no room for any kind of *should* or *ought*.

Even insofar as you have choice about the future, then it still isn't a matter of what *should* be but rather what *will* be—what you choose for it to be. And from the perspective of a human already in the future, or a god-like entity outside of time, it already is what you choose it to be. There is no sensible meaning in saying, "I *should* choose X instead of Y, but I *am* choosing Y." There is no sensible meaning in saying, "I *ought* to choose X instead of Y, but I *am* choosing Y."

When it comes to your choices, you always get exactly what you want, meaning what you choose.

Insofar as you do have the power of choice, it can feel overwhelming due to the open-ended freedom that comes with that—with there being multiple different equally right answers, answers essentially to the question, *what will you do?*

Your answer to that question is inherently true, inherently correct, and inherently right because it is your answer.

It can be a false comfort to falsely imagine the open-ended blank canvas of a question with infinite correct answers as instead being the non-nonsensical question of, *'what should I do?'* as if the right answer was already chosen and you just need to find and obey the chooser's commandment, as if it was a paint-by-the-numbers situation of rule-following instead of a blank canvas of infinite opportunities calling for free-spirited creativity.

Spiritual freedom is another term for self-discipline, and thus by extension it necessarily entails self-responsibility. George Bernard Shaw wrote, *"Liberty means self-responsibility, and that is why most men dread it."*

In a letter to his brother Theo, Vincent Van Gogh wrote the following:

> *"...how paralyzing it is, that stare of a blank canvas, which says to the painter: 'You can't do a thing.' The canvas has an idiotic stare and mesmerizes some painters so much that they turn into idiots themselves. Many painters are afraid in front of the blank canvas, but the blank canvas is afraid of the real, passionate painter who dares and who has broken the spell of 'you can't' once and for all.*
>
> *Life itself, too, is forever turning an infinitely vacant, dispiriting blank side towards man on which nothing appears, any more than it does on a blank canvas. But no matter how vacant and vain, how dead life may appear to be, the man of faith, of energy, of warmth, who knows something, will not be put off so easily. He wades in and does something and stays with it, in short, he violates, 'defiles' - they say."*

By letting go of false moralizing language, the false idea that life is merely some test upon which you must find the singular right answer lest you be naughty, you then realize that life is a blank canvas of infinite equally right possibilities upon which you choose to creatively and artistically create. You don't find the right answer; you create it. Whatever you choose to do becomes right—becomes true, becomes real, becomes part of reality, becomes revealed as seemingly fated all along—because you choose it.

Kierkegaard wrote, *"Anxiety is the dizziness of freedom."*

The cost of liberation from childish ideas of naughtiness and moralistic shame is mature self-responsibility. You don't have a bossy parent telling you what to do, holding your hand, choosing the path for you. Kierkegaard called it dizzying. Van Gogh described it as the paralyzing stare of a blank canvas.

Many humans turn from it. Many find comfort in spiritual slavery and lies. Many would choose slavery in a hell of lies over freedom because freedom is dizzying and uncomfortable, even overwhelming. Many would rather be considered naughty than be free. Many choose to sacrifice their freedom at the altar of addiction or imagine themselves as "shame-worthy" or "immoral" whatever that means rather than to admit they are free, shamelessly free, utterly, overwhelmingly free.

Let go of the slave morality and the comfortably anxious worrying about what *should* be, a fundamentally nonsensical pseudo-idea, and instead accept the dizzying sometimes uncomfortable blank canvas of all that can be, the beautiful sandbox of life, the grand art-piece that is reality.

You have the paintbrush in your hand. You are not a slave or test-taker, but an artist.

Suggestion Five — Let go of resentment, hate, and unforgiveness towards others, including your past self. Accept their choices, and accept them as they are.

I n his book, Stillness Speaks, Eckhart Tolle wrote the following:

"To let go of judgment does not mean that you don't see what they do. It means that you recognize their behavior as a form of conditioning, and you see it and accept it as that. You don't construct an identity out of it for that person.

That liberates you as well as the other person from identification with conditioning, with form, with mind.

[...]

If her past were your past, her pain your pain, her level of consciousness your level of consciousness, you would think and act exactly as she does. With this realization comes forgiveness, compassion, peace."

One can take the suggestion as meaning to *"unconditionally forgive others"*, which isn't necessarily wrong.

However, when you really and completely practice the acceptance of reality as it inexorably is, and thus accept others as they are and accept the choices of others as they are, then there is no need for forgiveness at all. There is nothing to forgive.

If you were fully in their shoes, you would do exactly as they do, so there is nothing to forgive. In fact, that idea is a necessary corollary of realizing that *the real you*, *the real me*, and *the real them* are identical, meaning three phrases for the same thing, the united singular essence of these diverse dancing forms.

In terms of *the real you*, you were, are, or will be in their shoes too, and you do, did, or will do exactly as they did or do. It was you. It is you. They are you.

From your perspective as an individual human being in his or her own here and now, other humans are the way they are. It's just a fact to accept as true, like the past as a whole. It's part of the unchangeable cards you are dealt. Do you need to forgive yesterday for being the way it was? Do you need to forgive the sky for raining or forgive the weather for being the way it is? Do mosquitoes need to be forgiven for liking blood? Ants for being dirty? The murderous lion for chasing the antelope? The antelope for running away and depriving the poor hungry lion of a meal?

Accepting the choices and the nature of other humans, other animals, and your past self is simply a specific case of accepting that which you cannot change or cannot control, of accepting unchangeable reality as it is.

Accepting the choices and nature of other humans and other aspects of unchangeable reality as a whole as the unchangeable cards you are dealt doesn't mean you don't then play those cards the best you can. Quite the opposite actually: accepting the cards with inner peace rather than wasting energy resenting or complaining about them being the way they inexorably are is necessary for playing the cards the best you can. Any of your finite time, energy, or resources put towards non-acceptance of the unchangeable (e.g. complaining, resentment, talking about *shoulds* and *oughts*, etc.) is thereby taken from putting that energy, time, or resources towards playing the cards the best you can.

It is only from a place of inner peace and acceptance that you can best play the cards you are dealt, meaning make your choices. It's by unconditionally accepting things as they are, including the choices of others, that you make your choices the best you can and thus find not only peace with your own choices as well as theirs.

Accepting the choices and the nature of other humans means completely letting go of resentment of unchangeable reality for being the way it is—which by extension includes unconditionally accepting the choices of others as being what they are, and unconditionally accepting others as they are, not as they 'should' be or such, whatever that would mean.

Insofar as the word 'should' even has meaning, then we must say that the past is exactly as it should be, everything that happened should have happened, and everything that should happen will happen.

Unconditional forgiveness—or more accurately the transcendence of the feeling that there ever really is anything to forgive—is the infinitely easy passive act of not making the mistake of looking at other people and thinking or saying, *"They shouldn't be the way they are,"* or *"They ought not have done what they did"*—nonsense utterances that would irrationally attempt to deny the simple fact that, whatever it is, it is what it is. People are what they are, and they did what they did. In this moment, in this body, those are the cards you are dealt.

Let go of the illusion that it could have been different. It couldn't have been different. The past couldn't have been different. The past can't be different. Rewind time and replay it infinite times, and it will turn out the exact same way every time. It couldn't have been different. It is what it is, forever, not just in time, but also outside of time in eternal reality.

Accept it. Love unchangeable reality as it is rather than bitterly and resentfully insisting it be or should be something different than what it inexorably is.

Accepting what you cannot control, and focusing squarely on what you can control (i.e. your choices in your unique present), is a matter of being honest with yourself about what you can and cannot do.

The past and the choices made by others are something you cannot control.

Resentment towards unchangeable things, particularly the past, can come from a foolish self-deceiving place of trying to control or change those uncontrollable and unchangeable things, of tricking yourself into thinking you are doing something—or trying to do something—you can't do. It's like shaking your fist at the sky to change the weather, but instead you wag your finger at the past and say *"Shame on you past; you should be different than you inexorably are!"*

Every second, penny, or bit of energy wasted on hateful resentment of that which you do not control is time, money, or energy stolen from yourself here and now. When you steal your own time or energy, you also steal and throw away your own inner peace.

Unconditional acceptance of what you do not control, including the nature and choices of other people and animals, costs nothing. It is the default. It is the passive. It is simply an absence of a certain form of expensive exhausting counter-productive wastefulness.

It is simply the letting go (a.k.a. liberating yourself) of the trap of wasting time, money, or energy on delusional futile unforgiveness. Unforgiving resentfulness is two mistakes in one: (1) thinking people have something to be forgiven for, and (2) not forgiving them for it.

Insofar as you feel people or things have to be forgiven for something, then forgive them. Forgive them unconditionally. Say, *"Even a rabid dog deserves unconditional love and forgiveness."*

It doesn't necessarily mean we don't put the dog in a cage. It doesn't necessarily mean we don't put the dog down. Those may be our cards to play, and only from a place of unconditional acceptance of that which we cannot control will we play the dealt cards (what we can control) the best we can such that we can be at peace with our choices too.

If practicing such unconditional forgiveness takes you to the point that you so unconditionally, instantly, and wholly accept people, animals, and things as they are that you no longer see there as being anything to forgive in the first place, then even better.

To engage in resentment is the choice to do something when doing nothing would preserve your inner peace.

Unforgiving hate and resentment seduce one away from the default of inner peace by motivating needless restless reality-denying doing.

Let go of hate. Liberate yourself from the burden of doing things based on hate. Love, acceptance, inner peace, and so-called forgiveness could not be easier. You don't need to try; you don't even need to do.

The only guaranteed victim of resentful hate is the hater.

The only one directly saved by unconditional love is the lover.

The one guaranteed to be made miserable by resentment is the resenter.

The one directly saved by forgiveness is the forgiver.

Hate and resentment are a poison the hater drinks.

There is great power in peacefulness and acceptance because there is great waste in restlessness, resentment, and unforgiveness.

Liberating oneself from unforgiving resentment and hate has a well-known correlation with incredible external abundance and material success. But of course! When you stop wasting your finite time, money, and energy complaining about and resenting the cards you are dealt, you suddenly have so much more time, money, and energy to put towards playing those cards the best you can, to put towards the art of living, and thus you indeed play those cards so much better.

For example, in a martial arts fight, the restless angry fighter who swings wildly tends to be easily defeated by the calm warrior who chooses his moves carefully, even stingily, who strategically uses his opponent's own restless force against him. It can even seem supernatural, the incredible power of calmness, of wu wei, of inner peace, of gracefulness, and of the spiritual liberation that is self-discipline.

Do not be disciplined by the siren song of hate and resentment that would seduce you into walking away from the luscious peaceful abundant lands of graceful self-disciplined invincible inner peace.

Choose the infinitely easier path of simply letting go of all the wasteful nonsense. Find yourself firmly planted in the empowering abundance-manifesting lands of inner peace, acceptance, forgiveness, and love. Those beautiful lands are always there for you, always waiting for you, always ready for you. The choice is yours, and when it comes to your choices, you always get what you want, meaning what you choose.

Suggestion Six —
Let go of possessiveness.

Your ego is mortal. You are not your ego.

Your body is mortal. You are not your body.

You are the essence, not the form, not the human form, not any form. You are not the clothes, the car, the house, the body, the brain, the memory, the title, the job, the bank account. Even more, you cannot keep these things, and in a sense you do not really ever own things, any thing. You may be driving a car inside a body for now, but ultimately those things, both the body and the car, will be returned to the sands of time, as sands—mere dust—themselves.

In their many forms, attachment, clinginess, and possessiveness are ultimately all based on a doomed delusion: that the impermanent is permanent.

For example, romantic possessiveness may drive you to stop your spouse from having an affair, or to murder their lover if they do, but regardless you will still lose that spouse eventually. They may get hit by a bus next week, or may leave you for another lover next year, or they may die of cancer in ten years. All marriages, even the happiest ones, end in divorce or death.

Clingy attachment and possessiveness entails denying or fighting a fundamental unavoidable truth: *Everything that has a beginning has an end. Everything that is created in time is destroyed in time. Everything that is born will die.*

Your love story with your spouse will end one day. The story of your human life will end one day. That human child you tuck into bed at night will die one day.

161

You are not living with integrity when you lie to yourself. You are not acting with integrity when you make choices based on self-deception, based on lies you tell yourself.

The car, the house, the money, the clothes... It will all be taken from you one day somehow. It is all at most borrowed, very briefly borrowed. It will all be returned. It will all be returned to dust, as will the human you see in the mirror. The human you see in the mirror will be dead in less than the blink of a cosmic eye.

In an official OnlineBookClub.org interview, author David J Mauro said the following:

"I now realize that a person who feels they have nothing left to lose is a fantastic and dangerous soul. In such moments we are bulletproof in a sense."

There are two ways to get to that bulletproof point: one is to lose everything that you think matters to you through some series of unfortunate events, but the other is to learn to let go, to give up possessiveness completely, to choose to appreciate rather than cling, to realize nothing is ever really yours to own.

If you think you own the sun and have a right to its beauty, you will cry or scream at the sunset. But when you realize you have nothing to lose because you never really own anything in the first place, then you love both the sunrise and the sunset, and the very fleetingness of things contributes to their beauty: each moment unique, each dance its own. Each hug, each kiss, each smile, rising and setting, floating away.

To love is very different than to own. Admire and appreciate without clinging, without desperate possessiveness. Just love, true unpossessive love.

One day when you tuck your beloved child into bed, it will be the last time you do, for one reason or another. Accepting that inevitable fact each time you tuck in the child—whether it later turns out to be the last or not—makes the moment so much sweeter and precious, like a one-of-a-kind collector item. Even if you have 100 times left to kiss and hug that child, or your beloved spouse, you gain so much by savoring each time like it was the last.

Even if you knew it was not the last time but rather the second to last time or third to last time that you would ever hug or kiss your beloved child or beloved spouse, would you not still savor it and be utterly present for it? Imagine that you suddenly found you would only get to hug your beloved spouse or child two more times ever, meaning the next time would be second to last but not last. How would you treat that second to last hug? Would you treat the second to last much differently than the last? The mistake we often make is to treat it as if we have infinite left when we have so few. Even a hundred or thousand is so few, too few to not cherish each like it was the last.

Ram Dass once wisely said, *"Our journey is about being more involved in life, and yet less attached to it."*

By letting go of the delusion that you can forever possess that which you cannot possess or forever keep that which cannot be kept, and by being honest with yourself about how time will quickly strip these things from your human grasp, you gain so much in the present moment. You savor each hug, each kiss, each dance like it was the last. And, in a sense, each is indeed its own last—you discover—because each is one of a kind and filled with infinite unique beauty. When you savor each hug, each kiss, each beautiful moment like it is the last, you thereby have the presence and attitude of gratitude that lets you see the uniqueness and detail of the special one-of-kind moment, the first and last of its kind.

When your hands stop clinging in desperate futile denial-ridden attachment, they become free to truly behold the literally *awesome* infinite beauty of each passing moment in the eternal present.

By letting go of future-oriented delusions that would have you sacrifice savoring the present for a fictional future, we discover an awe-inspiring eternity in the present, an infinite well of beauty in the unique overwhelmingly real present moment.

It is the seemingly magical here-and-now, the space-and-time-transcending pseudo-place where we find *the real you*, where we find *presence* itself, where we find *here-and-nowness* itself, where we find that which is undeniably realer and more fundamental than space or time or even spacetime. It is where we find *you*, the eternal real *you*, the beauty in the eye of the beholder and the beholder of all beauty.

*Suggestion Seven — Let go of
the false idolization of
positivity and superficial
happiness. Accept the shadow
of all things including yourself.*

Carl Jung wrote, "How can I be substantial if I do not cast a shadow? I must have a dark side also If I am to be whole."

There is nothing wrong with wanting to spread love and light. When your heart bursts with joy and love, you may want to run around shaking your fellow humans by the shoulders to spread the good news.

However, positivity becomes toxic when it entails dishonest denial.

Inner peace does not mean you never cry, you never bleed, you never hurt, you never feel fear, feel anger, or feel pain.

Instead, when you accept that you will experience and feel all of those things, and accept everything, then you have inner peace even when you cry, even when you bleed, even when you hurt.

Then, it becomes clearer to see that in many ways the great life is the life filled with blood, sweat, and tears, and that you wouldn't have it any other way. You may say then that *a dry life without tears* is the one not worth living. You may say then that the lifeless unmoving rollercoaster is the one not worth riding, and that it is not really a rollercoaster at all, that it is essentially nothing at all. Pure bliss is neither bliss nor anything because it is pure nothingness. The yin and the yang alone are lifeless and thus rendered equal. True beauty, meaning, and lifefulness—existence—transcend duality. It is not in the yin or the yang, but in the way the yin dances with the yang. It is not in the light or the dark, but in the way the light dances with the dark. It is not in the ups or the downs of the track, but the way they dance together to make a ride at all. It is not in the good cards or the bad cards, but in the art and dance of playing the cards that requires both. It is not in the success or failure, but in the artful dance of opportunity and challenge.

Perhaps you can then even earnestly say, if it's up to you, the more blood, sweat, and tears, the better.

Inner peace doesn't mean outer peace, and if total consistent outer peace was obtainable or even truly desirable, then inner peace wouldn't be needed or useful.

A crucial aspect of the beauty of life and of the beautiful struggle that unites us is that it isn't all smiles and rainbows. Sometimes it's the tears we share and the painful hugs. With inner peace, the challenges act as opportunities. But then, even more, it is revealed that, without challenge, there is no chance for opportunity at all.

Accept and love the dark side of life too. If you look in the mirror and see a human with tears in his or her eyes, or a bloody smile, love that human just the same, more maybe.

Just love it all.

Just love everything.

Suggestion Eight —
Embrace discomfort.
Let go of comfort addiction.

The comfort zone is a sticky trap, a seductive cage.

To truly overcome temptation is to transcend comfort, to become immune to the seductive siren song of the comfort zone. This doesn't mean you stop feeling comfort or even that you stop desiring comfort, but rather that you approach comfort and approach desire like a brave person approaches fear.

Embrace discomfort. Embrace your freedom from the hellish bliss of ignorance.

If the truth hurts the body and ego, then laugh in disobedient glee as the honest truth beats you bloody.

In such disobedience, one finds not only freedom but a form of invincibility. A spirit with nothing to lose is the most powerfully free spirit of all. Letting go is empowering. Those who cling possessively to comfort become themselves possessed, possessed not only by the comfort zone but also by the futility of the never-ending rat race, of the hamster wheel, of the need and desire to always have more: more food, more money, more fame, a bigger house, a fluffier bed. Comfort isn't contentment, and unlike the consistent contentment of inner peace, comfort is always fleeting.

What you own has a way of owning you, and thus the more you hoard, the more of a prisoner you become.

The only true ownership is self-ownership, not ownership of the body or fleeting mortal ego, but rather ownership of who and what you really are, ownership of the one thing that is truly worth anything: That is you and the freedom of your spirit.

"For what has a man profited if he gains the world for the price of his soul?"

With free-spirited inner peace, one is content while sweating in pain on a treadmill, content while having a drink in a crowded bar or while sitting alone sober at home, content while rich and content while poor. With inner peace, one is free from the cyclical fickle compulsions of discontent's restless insatiable hunger. Those with inner peace are content when hungry, content when full, content in discomfort, and content when comforted, content in pain, content in pleasure. They bring heaven with them wherever they go, even on a cold journey up a mountain or into a boxing ring. Even in a cancer ward or a war zone, they have grace under fire no matter the fire. That is true grace. The inner peace of spiritual liberation is in that way an invincible saving grace.

When you have inner peace, the grass is always so beautifully green no matter where you go. When you have inner peace, the grass is always green enough on this side, the side on which you find yourself. From the clear-minded place of content inner peace and spiritual freedom, you are inspired to water the grass on which you stand, to dance upon it, to sit in stillness upon it, or to journey happily to other grass, but whatever it is you are inspired to do or not do is inspired from a place content free-spirited inner peace, not an insatiable discontent addiction to comfort or the false belief that the heaven of true contentment exists only in the future. With the spiritual freedom (a.k.a. self-discipline) and inner peace found in the present and in presence itself, heaven is all around you everywhere you look.

The beautiful heaven you may see is the heaven you carry with you, and in a way that beautiful heaven is you. The world you see is mostly a mirror. You are the projector projecting on the would-be blank reflective screen. When you see clearly into that mirror, you will see beauty.

Suggestion Nine — Let go of future idolization. Embrace the present.

What does it mean to be more present? What are the benefits of living in the present? What does it mean to live in the present and accept the present with free-spirited inner peace?

People who do not have healthy self-esteem in the present, or who do not properly esteem the present, have a special propensity for creating false idols out of their future self or the future itself. Nonetheless, all humans tend to do it to some varying degree, meaning to devalue the very real present and overvalue the imagined future.

For just one of infinite examples, consider a human who lives in the so-called *first world*, finding themselves on the luckier side of this "tale of two cities". This person's material conditions far exceed the material wealth and creature comforts of the average human on the planet not only in the modern age but even more so if the conditions of past humans are considered. Most humans never had the pleasure of enjoying the invention of the toilet and modern plumbing. Nonetheless, it would not be unusual for that seemingly very lucky human to lack inner peace and discontentedly tell themselves, maybe while ungratefully sitting on their toilet, *"Once I make a million dollars, then I will finally be happy and at peace,"* or, *"Once I lose 20 lbs, then I will finally be happy and at peace,"* or, *"Once I get married and have kids, then I will finally be happy and at peace."*

Or, perhaps, *"Once I get divorced from this selfish jerk and get to enjoy being single again, then I will finally be happy and at peace."*

Or, perhaps they don't want a divorce. Perhaps they say, *"Once my selfish immature jerk of a spouse grows up, takes self-responsibility, and starts acting right, then I can finally be happy and at peace."*

"Once this pain in my leg goes away, I can finally be happy and at peace."

"Once I get a new career, I can finally be happy and at peace."

Instead of looking around with gratitude and awe at all things to be grateful for in their present including the one under their butt, they look to an imaginary future of not only greener grass but grass that is finally going to be green enough one day allegedly.

But now imagine this human wins a million-dollar lottery or otherwise makes a million bucks, and loses the 20 lbs. Then, it would be common for him to still be discontent and lack inner peace, carrying to the future the same ungracious habits that have been denying him inner peace. Then as a millionaire sitting on a solid gold toilet, he might say, *"Once I make a **billion** dollars, then I will be happy."* And if it's not more money, it will be something else. Now he needs a girlfriend, or a new one because the one he has isn't good enough anymore. Comfort is fleeting, and there is always more of it to get.

You cannot reach a state of desirelessness by fulfilling your desires. You can not reach a state of goallessness by achieving your current goals. If you define happiness as having no unachieved goals, and wait to have inner peace until you achieve all your goals and fulfill your desires, it will never happen. That's a future that does not exist, that cannot exist.

This process of trying to get to that living heaven on Earth by feeding the insatiable body and ego, of foolishly trying to actually satiate it, is called the *hedonic treadmill.*

Inner peace does not exist at the end of the hedonic treadmill, nothing does, because indeed the end of that treadmill does not exist. It is a treadmill to nowhere but an impossible fictional future. In reality, the actual future to which it will take you is just as lacking in inner peace as your present if not more.

But such silly future idolization makes for a cleverly self-deceptive excuse for choosing to forgo inner peace in the present, your here and now.

In other words, humans self-abuse in large part by rationalizing their chosen discontent in the present—their here and now—as being in service of or sacrifice to some future self or future cause, often mislabeling it as "love" in some cyclical pseudo-loving "love-hate" relationship with their own so-called future self.

In the false name of true conscious love, human beings abuse themselves in the present and dishonestly rationalize their inner-peace-sacrificing choices in the present with all sorts of muddy egotistical mental acrobatics.

We are each 100% in control of our choices. When it comes to our choices, we always get exactly what we want, meaning what we choose. But despite those aforementioned repeat-worthy facts, humans are capable of the following:

(1) choosing one thing and claiming they want (or *"should be doing"*) the other

(2) claiming they don't have a choice when they do (e.g. "I *need* some comfort, so I *have* to eat"; "It was a long day, so I *need* a drink.")

173

(3) pretending they do have a choice when they don't (e.g. trying to change the past or otherwise not accepting that the past is what it is).

The inner peace of spiritual freedom (a.k.a. self-discipline) is yours for the taking in the present, and only ever in the present, but many humans choose not to take it, with one of the most common lies or rationalizations for that sad choice being that they are sacrificing their happiness in the present for the sake of their future self, the epitome of self-abuse, of being in a toxic abusive relationship with their selves over time.

Whether we talk of abusive relationships with oneself over time, or between two different humans in space, there is a simple truth that reveals a fundamental fallacy in the dishonest mental acrobatics used to rationalize the fact that one isn't at peace with their choices in the present despite being 100% in control of those choices. That simple revealing truth is this:

*True love is **not** sacrificing your happiness for another; true love is being happy to sacrifice.*

If the so-called sacrifices you are making for someone else, including your future self, do not bring you the contentment of inner peace in the present, *right here, right now*, then they are not loving sacrifices, not in the sense of true conscious love.

If the so-called sacrifices you are making for someone else, including your future self, require you to give up your spiritual freedom or inner peace, *right here, right now*, then they are not loving sacrifices, not in the sense of true conscious love.

By all means, if you truly love your future self, or another human across space, please do feel free to eagerly, happily, and bravely embrace pain, fear, or discomfort as a loving sacrifice, but note that in such a case the loving sacrifice makes you truly happy, in the present, in the sense of your inner peace and spiritually liberated contentment.

If it's true conscious love, you will be happy to be giving, happy to be sacrificing, even through pain, loss, discomfort, sweat, tears, and blood.

If you are on a treadmill sweating in pain out of true love for your future self, then you will have content inner peace even while feeling that pain and sweat. You will be happy to be giving that gift to your future self. You will be doing it because it makes you happy in the sense of inner peace in the present, because it is what you truly want in the present. It will be an expression of your spiritual freedom, of you choosing what you really want, *right here, right now.*

Future-oriented goals can be useful to the degree they act like a guiding North Star in the sky to help you in the present, a meeting point between the sky and the ground on the horizon to navigate you on your journey. But the journey never ends; it is inexorably Sisyphustic. You never reach that North Star. Albert Camus wrote, *"One must imagine Sisyphus happy."*

If you say, *"I will finally be happy and at peace once I make a million dollars,"* it is a lie you tell yourself while in a toxic if not abusive relationship with your future self, a dishonest excuse for your discontent in the present as being in the service of your future millionaire self.

If you say, *"I will finally be happy and at peace once I reach my goal weight,"* it is a lie you tell yourself while in a dishonest toxic abusive relationship with your future fitter self.

If you say, *"I will finally be happy and at peace once I get to the bar and have a drink,"* it is a lie.

If you say, *"I will finally be happy and at peace once I suffer through the next 365 days of inner-peace-lacking misery and earn my one-year sobriety chip,"* it is a lie.

Such dishonest inner-peace-lacking mental talk not only rationalizes and motivates one to sacrifice their inner peace and spiritual freedom (a.k.a. self-discipline) in the present, but also helps rationalize one's upcoming choice to unsurprisingly deviate from their alleged goal. If the person is discontent and constantly blames that discontent on the diet or on the fact that they are walking the path to the alleged goal, whatever it is, then of course the person will almost certainly deviate from that path and not even achieve the goal in the long-term.

A discontent person lacking inner peace who believes that happenstance and external circumstances such as making money, losing weight, or earning a sobriety chip will make them finally content one day in the future will generally not successfully walk that path to that future because they would have to walk it discontentedly, in inner-peace-lacking misery day after day. If you aren't happy to be on the treadmill sweating in pain, then you are unlikely to stay on it very long. If you are with inner peace happy to sacrifice for your future self out of true love, happy to embrace pain and discomfort on that treadmill out of true love for future self, then you will be much more likely to stay on it and continue enjoying that true happiness of love that is called inner peace and deeply linked to spiritual freedom (a.k.a. self-discipline).

It's in that very sense that sobriety can be as much a false idol to an alcoholic as alcohol. It's in that very sense that having a sculpted beach body in an imaginary future can be as much of a false idol to an overeating food addict as the food and the fleeting comfort of binge eating.

Discontent people imagine that contentment is found on the greener grass of the other side, which is always at least slightly in the future. But the contentment of inner peace and spiritual freedom (a.k.a. self-discipline) is never found in the greener grass of the future. It is always and only available in the present, *right here, right now*, no greener grass needed.

The discontent person lacking inner peace will be discontent while drinking and while sober, and hence they are likely to bounce between the two in a cycle of misery. The discontent person lacking inner peace will be discontent while binge eating and while sticking to their diet; thus they are likely to bounce between the two in a cycle of misery, desperately trying to find the key to happiness or at least something to self-medicate them with a bit of comfort in their persistent misery, the misery of not having inner peace, of not being in a truly loving relationship with their selves over time and across space built on true conscious love.

In contrast, the unwavering contentment of inner peace is conducive to decisiveness, determination, consistency, goal-achievement, and success in the self-directed open-world game of life. There is an art—*a deeply meaningful, creative, powerful art*—in happily chasing success as a free-spirited (a.k.a. self-disciplined) human being with inspired inner peace because you—*an inspired free-spirited entity*—choose and creatively create the very goals that define the chased success. The art and contentment of that special kind are in the chasing itself—the playing of the endless game. With that approach, one often has this attitude: *the harder the game, the better*. In analogy, an artistic sculptor might look for a rock to be sculpted and think, *the bigger the better*. To such a sculptor, external heaven might be imagined as a sisyphustic world with an infinitely big rock that allows for infinite sculpting, infinite creative playing of the challenging game, infinite happy sweating, bleeding, and blistering.

Feel free to seek greener grass insofar as the seeking itself provides inner peace and contentment in the present, meaning insofar as you enjoy the journey with content inner peace. You make your conscious choices only in the present, the *here and now*. Yes, a true conscious lover will often make amazing sacrifices (in the present) for the one they consciously love, but those loving sacrifices make the lover happy at the time and place of sacrifice, happy in the sense of maintaining inner peace and spiritual freedom. It's the spiritual happiness of being at peace with your choices in the present, which is something that nobody and nothing can take from you nor force upon you.

Your future-oriented goals at any given time are relative to that present and at best merely help guide you on the ways you can contently enjoy inner peace in that present, often by lovingly sacrificing for your future self out of true conscious love if you so choose, which you will indeed likely choose to do if it makes you truly happy in the present to do, in terms of your inner peace and the contentment of spiritual liberation.

For example, imagine, you are in the gym working out very hard and exercising great self-discipline (a.k.a. spiritual liberation), your body dripping in sweat, your muscles painfully sore and throbbing, and you say to yourself, *"This pain feels so freaking good!"*

Then, indeed, you may be in a healthy loving relationship with your future self, and probably all of humanity, assuming you have inner peace.

One with inner peace and the invincible contentment of spiritual freedom (a.k.a. self-discipline) is often very happy to embrace discomfort, to embrace delicious pain and exciting fear.

Spiritually speaking, fear, discomfort, hunger, and pain can all feel so deliciously good at a spiritual level when truly chosen with true love as a spiritually liberated person, rather than as some petty prop in an act of self-deceiving paradoxically voluntary spiritual slavery at the abusive altar of some false idol. For many, that false idol is the future self. For many, the false idol whose altar at which they sacrifice their inner peace, contentment, and spiritual freedom is the future and the imagined happiness that it contains, once all goals have been achieved, once all destinations have been reached.

What quicker way to not enjoy the endless journey than by falsely idolizing some unreachable imaginary end?

It's hard to imagine Sisyphus happy if he falsely thinks he can get the boulder securely on top of the hill, and thinks that unreachable place is the only place where contentment and inner peace exist.

The spiritual freedom that is self-discipline does not entail being an unhappy pseudo-slave to your future self. That is the antithesis of spiritual liberation. That is the antithesis of the invincible inner peace of self-discipline. That is the antithesis of the utter spiritual joy and salvation of realizing and manifesting the true conscious love that is *the real you* and the recognition of your literal undeniable oneness with the consciousness of all other conscious beings.

By all means, recognize your oneness with other human beings, perhaps with all life, perhaps with the whole universe. By all means, love all other conscious people including your future self, but in doing so please remember that true love does not cause the lover to sacrifice inner peace or self-discipline. Rather, the opposite is true: The behaviors and feelings of true love are what naturally emerge from a conscious person who is peacefully contently spiritually liberated.

Love is what comes out when you, *the real you*, are set free.

Meister Eckhart wrote,

"The most important hour is always the present. The most significant person is precisely the one sitting across from you right now. The most necessary work is always love."

Suggestion Ten — Let go of restlessness and overcommitment. Do less, better.

Albert Einstein wrote, "A calm and modest life brings more happiness than the pursuit of success combined with constant restlessness."

Carl Jung wrote, *"People will do anything, no matter how absurd, in order to avoid facing their own souls. They will practice Yoga and all its exercises, observe a strict regimen of diet, learn the literature of the whole world - all because they cannot get along with themselves and have not the slightest faith that anything useful could ever come out of their own soul."*

As was discussed in more detail earlier in this book, anxious restlessness is a symptom of discontentment, or in other words of a lack of inner peace and spiritual freedom. Granted, such inner peace and spiritual freedom (a.k.a. self-discipline) often does—essentially by definition—entail a form of unanxious motivating free-spirited *inspiration*. But there is a grace and gracefulness to such *inspired* action, such that even a boxer or literal fighter in the zone is something of a graceful artist who beautifully manifests the incredible power of inner peace and spiritual freedom. Even in the midst of the throwing of literal punches and splashing of literal blood, one can see in the rapid and complex activity a graceful harmony and flow. That is, at least, when the athlete or martial artist acts from a place of inspired free-spirited inner peace.

The discontentment and resentment that motivate anxious restlessness doesn't merely result in the symptom that is restless overdoing, but also and perhaps even more destructively it also results in overpromising and thus failing to deliver all that is promised, be it promised to others or to oneself. What ends up being overdone is the promising and pledging itself, but what's promised and pledged to be done isn't actually done.

The gracefulness of the free-spirited (a.k.a. self-disciplined) person is manifested as *doing without trying*. So it is no surprise that the opposite of such spiritual freedom and inner peace is often manifested as *trying without doing*. Or, actually, often that is *promising and pledging without doing*.

It's a funny irony that in various walks of life the self-disciplined free-spirited non-restless person will often tend to achieve more success, tend to be more effective, and tend to get more done than the anxious discontent addiction-prone restless person. As ironic as it may be, the productivity addict often tends to be less productive than the one who acts from a place of content inner peace. The calm warrior with inner peace will often easily defeat the recklessly restless and anxious one. That is both in fact and in metaphor. The dog that barks the most often has the weakest bite. And indeed it is likely that you will never see a dog bark and bite at the same time. Those who most talk the talk are typically too busy talking to walk the walk.

Generally speaking, what matters most is what you do, not what you say you will do. Actions speak infinitely louder than words. Like a barking dog, those who 'try' to do the most or claim they will do the most often actually don't succeed at much of anything. They may 'try' to juggle a lot well, but they 'try' without actually doing.

It's easy to say, *"I'll start dieting next Monday,"* while you stuff your face with greasy chips.

It's easy to say to a spouse or lover, *"you are my one and only"*, but much fewer will live it.

It's easy to say you love yourself, but then what have you actually done? Ask yourself, how have I loved myself today? What did I do that is a manifestation of my love for myself?

It's easy to say you love your spouse, your kids, your best friend, or your literal neighbor. But how have you loved them today? What have you actually done?

Think of the parent who says they love their drug-addicted child, but still enables the child by giving the child money when the child asks.

Think of the domestic abuser who gets on his or her knees crying claiming to love their lover after beating the person bloody the night before.

Think of the partner or roommate that lays on the couch texting you, *"I love you,"* from their smartphone while the sink is overflowing with dishes and the trash can is bubbling over with gross smelly unwitting science experiments.

What have you actually done lately? What sacrifices have you made today?

Careful with these questions; don't overintend or overpromise the doing because that's a recipe for failure and stress.

Bark less.

Promise less.

Commit less.

Do less, better.

Do without trying instead of trying to do too much.

You can keep the few promises you do make by only making a few. You can more likely win the battles you choose to fight by choosing your battles carefully and stingily.

The irony of becoming the kind of human who actually in a sense does more—meaning succeeds more, accomplishes more, and achieves more and manifests love more—is that a crucial element is becoming the kind of human who intends to do less and who promises to do less. By juggling less, you juggle better. By juggling less, you can more easily juggle with grace, inner peace, and self-discipline (a.k.a. freedom of spirit).

In contrast, by juggling too much, you end up not juggling anything at all.

It's easy to get a sudden wake-up call or jolt of emotional motivation and then promise the world to yourself or others. *"I'll never do drugs again," "I'll never cheat on my diet again," "I'll never cheat on my spouse again,"* or *"Starting today, I'll work out in the gym every single day for the rest of my life."*

But by excessively promising, you are increasing the chances of failure. At a certain point of overpromising, you guarantee failure. You can only do so much and spread yourself so thin. You can only juggle so much.

There is a reason that recovering addicts find such help in wise catch phrases such as *"one day at a time"* and *"relapse is a part of recovery"*. We can all benefit from these because all humans are on the addiction spectrum.

The damage from overpromising is a double hit: First, making the dishonest promise is in and of itself problematic. But then the actual breaking of a promise has its own separate effects, including but not limited to feelings of guilt and shame, as well as gaining a reputation of being unreliable.

For example, you can overpromise to yourself, "*I'll never eat cookies again.*" Then likely you will eventually cave and eat one cookie from the bag. At that point, you might feel awful for breaking your promise, and you might hate yourself for it. Then, in tears and self-loathing misery, you may say "*f--- it*", and eat the rest of the bag of cookies, if not simply as a small self-medicating comfort in your self-loathing misery. But what was the more influential factor: Eating one measly cookie or promising yourself you would never eat a cookie ever again?

The more you envision being some unrealistically perfect version of yourself in the future, the more you make yourself feel bad in the present, and the more you abusively put pressure and unfair expectations on your future self. It's a clandestine way of putting yourself down. You set an impossible standard and then compare yourself to it and feel bad.

The more you spread yourself too thin, the worse you do everything.

The more you try to juggle, the more likely you accidentally drop everything.

Sometimes it's better to succeed at one thing than fail at many.

Sometimes it's preferable to do one thing great, with stubborn determination, than do many things poorly and half-assed.

The goal isn't necessarily to make no commitments at all, but to keep the commitments you make. That goes for commitments to other people as well as to yourself.

Needless to say, someone who trusts themself to keep their commitments and promises will be much more careful about making such promises. To use finances as both an analogy and a metaphor for the broader concept, someone who reliably pays their financial debts will be more careful about taking out high-interest loans. Accordingly, a useful motto or rule of thumb is as follows:

Make fewer commitments, but keep more of the commitments you make.

Choose your battles, stingily. Do less, better.

Restlessness and the urge to overcommit or overdo can entail having a rushed voice in one's head, pretending to be oneself, that constantly and loudly asks with desperate anxiety, *"What should I do?! What are they telling me I ought to do?! What must I do?! What am I doing wrong?! I need to get better; how do I get better?! I'm bad; how can I be good?! What do I need to do to be right?! What ought I be doing that I am not doing?! I need to know what I need to do so that I can do it and stop being such a shameful guilty naughty loser! Ah, I'm a fat gross lazy piece of crap!"*

Insofar as one identifies with such an anxious rushed egoic voice, one will not have inner peace.

The body and ego are selfish, greedy, insatiable, and constantly anxious.

Laziness can be a major prop in some people's insatiable comfort addiction or spiritual slavery, but many times the opposite—*anxious restlessness*—is the more deeply rooted and influential issue. That's because the primitive body and ego are so naturally desperate, fearful, greedy, selfish, and insatiable. They want to live forever, but they will die, probably very soon. They desperately want to be comfortable and satiated, but they never fully are. Humans are much more like rushed anxious squirrels than they usually admit. In the same way that humans often overeat to the point of morbid obesity, so too do they often overcommit and overborrow to the point of excessive debt, both financial and otherwise. In both cases there is a temporal selfishness to such self-abuse, since it is the future human who pays the price of the debt, be it literally financial or more broadly speaking.

The ego will lie. The egoic voice in your head pretending to be you will lie. It may say:

"It was a hard day, so I need to eat for comfort."

"I must eat."

"I need a drink of whiskey."

"I want to not gamble, but I have to go to the casino one last time."

"I can't quit until I'm ahead."

"I need to win the money I lost before I can stop."

"I need one last fix before I go to rehab."

"I need a spouse because I cannot be happy living alone."

"I have to do something."

"They need to be punished."

"I have to teach them a lesson."

"The world sucks; I need to fix it."

"I can't be happy with inner peace until the world is fixed!"

"I need to do something! What should I do? OMG, what do I do?!"

Take a breath. Slow your mind's thoughts. If you cannot turn off the monologue in your brain pretending to be you, take a step back, so it's just a little less loud. Take a breath, so it's a little less fast.

Find the space between the words.

Can you slow the voice in your head?

Trying to turn it off can just add to the anxiety. Telling it to shut up just adds another voice to the overcrowded loud mix. If you can, just slow it down, or take a step back, or notice that the silence is still beneath the noise, between the words, even when they are fast and loud. It may tend to be easier to see the silence between and behind them when the thoughts and words are slower and quieter, but the silence is always still there, that conscious omnipresent silence, that non-verbal awareness and source of *presence itself* which is *the real you*.

Nothing needs to be done that isn't done. Nothing should be done that isn't done. Nothing ought to be done that isn't done.

When it comes to the inner-peace-stealing needless suffering of needless anxiety, sometimes it isn't just about the speed of the thoughts or the loudness of the thoughts, but the tone. It can be the false sense of direness or over-urgency. On this topic, consider the following wise words of Osho:

> "I don't think existence wants you to be serious. I have not seen a serious tree. I have not seen a serious bird. I have not seen a serious starry night. It seems they are all laughing in their own ways, dancing in their own ways. We may not understand it, but there is a subtle feeling that the whole of existence is a celebration."

Alan Watts once said a similar thing:

"Man suffers only because he takes seriously what the gods made for fun."

You only have this human body for a very little bit.

As a human, if you spend your whole life anxiously rushing around with loud rushing thoughts in your brain, you rush only to your inevitable death.

That is reason enough to slow down and smell the proverbial flowers.

Stop, if you can; stop and smell those flowers.

The peace is always there, underneath the play pretend. You are always there. The silence between the words is always there.

The Karmic Payoff of Doing Less Better

Some debts are financial; many are not. All are karmic, meaning inherited.

Each night you die, and each morning you are reborn. You are reborn in a similar image but not the exact same image. You are reborn in a similar body, but not the exact same body.

You inherit the debts of the dead, and the checks you write today—both figurative and literal—are passed on as debts to your child tomorrow.

When it comes to making commitments and promises, it is an act of kind loving charity to be stingy. Even at the risk of appearing lazy or unkind to other humans in space—meaning your other selves across space—it is your other selves across time that you sneakily and greedily throw under the bus to selfishly snatch up the false good karma of overpromising to your peers today.

It isn't solely debt, war, and addiction that you pass on to your children. It's also the freedom from the addictive cycles you break. It's the peace from the wars you don't start, and the wars you end. It's the friends you make. It's the petals of the flowers you plant. It's the fruit of the trees you keep.

The inertia of karmic cycles goes both ways. Smiles are as contagious as frowns.

What wars will you start today? What peace will you keep? What debts will you incur and which will you settle? What will you mow? What will you sow?

For your children tomorrow, both literal and figurative, what seeds will you plant today?

Suggestion Eleven — Just Love Everything and Everyone

When it comes to other people, including but not limited to the younger and older versions of the human you see in the mirror, love involves truly seeing yourself in another, seeing your irrevocable inner greatness in another, and working together to further actualize your shared self.

Your relationship to the human you see in the mirror as contrasted to other humans besides that human is analogous to the relationship between a parent and their young child versus other children not in their care. In other words, it's analogous to the difference between your relationship to your own proverbial backyard versus your relationship to someone else's backyard. Some say to clean your own proverbial backyard first, but we can take that advice further and realize our backyard could always be cleaned further. In form, neither our own proverbial backyard, nor our own children, nor our own parenting, nor the human we see in the mirror are ever perfect. There is always more cleaning to do. There is always more parenting to do. There is always more self-reflection to do. There is always more self-actualization to do. The imperfect form always clothes the perfect essence, the beautiful perfect united essence that is *the real you* and by extension *the real us*. So clean your backyard not merely *first*, but in a sense also *only*.

That is proverbial, of course. If someone assertively asks you to help them clean their literal backyard or such, of course you can choose to help them if you want to help them out of love and kindness.

However, generally speaking, it isn't love or kindness that would have you shove your so-called help down someone else's throat, be that someone else in space or time, often simply as a way to distract yourself from how messy your own proverbial backyard may be and how much the human you see in the mirror needs your help *right here right now.*

Many would wastefully or counterproductively point their finger at others (including their past self) and say what those others should do or should have done, rather than look at the human in the mirror and think about what that person in the mirror can do and then simply decide what to do out of all those countless things one can do, in this seemingly magical thing that is the present moment, the *here and now.*

Many would read a book like this and think, *this would be great advice for my spouse to follow; how do I get my spouse to obey this advice?! If only my spouse would follow this advice, then things would be better and lovable, and I would finally be happy.*

Many would read this book and think, *this would be great advice for my neighbor to follow; how do I get my neighbor to obey this advice? If only my neighbor would follow this advice, then things would be better and lovable, and I would finally be happy.*

Many would read this book and think, *this would be great advice for my literal parents to follow; how do I get my parents to obey this advice? If only my parents would follow this advice, then things would be better and lovable, and I would finally be happy.*

If you think the advice is good to follow, then follow it yourself. If not, then don't.

To think others *should* follow it or to believe they need to follow it, is to hypocritically not follow it yourself. If you don't think it's good advice for you to follow, then don't, but if you do think it's good advice to follow, then follow it by accepting others as they are and unconditionally loving them as they are. There is nothing they need to do or change for you to have inner peace right here right now. There is nothing they need to do or change for you to enjoy the wonderful invincible contentment of spiritual freedom (a.k.a. self-discipline) right here right now.

Even the meanest and most unkind people don't need to start loving everything for you to love everything including them. They don't need to change a thing for you to have inner peace and spiritual freedom (a.k.a. self-discipline).

It will never ever be your place to decide what your neighbors in time or space *should* do. That is the nature of *self*-discipline (a.ka. spiritual freedom). That is the nature of inner peace. It comes from within and only within.

Spiritual freedom (a.k.a. self-discipline) can never be forced on another, nor can it ever be withheld from another. It is yours and yours alone to give to or withhold from *only* the human you see in the mirror in the present moment, the eternal now.

Love others exactly as they are, unconditionally. Love everything, unconditionally. Resent nothing real. Nobody and nothing needs to be different or do anything different for you to have the invincible contentment of inner peace and spiritual freedom (self-discipline). If from a place of inner peace and content free-spirited self-discipline you behave in loving kind ways, such as by giving certain forms of help to those who explicitly ask for it or at least consent to it, you do so because that makes you happy because of who you are and who you choose to be in the present moment you choose such actions.

As a practical rule of thumb, you cannot help someone who doesn't want to help themselves, and what you might consider help might not even be help for them.

In analogy, you might like peanut butter and like to often have it as a healthy snack. To someone with a peanut allergy, it's poison. Don't force your beloved peanut butter on others.

You can love your peanut butter while still loving those who don't eat peanut butter. If it's a mistake for them to not eat, then it's their mistake to make, but it may not be a mistake at all. The apparent or alleged mistakes of others are beautiful in their own way, in part because, as said so often, the beauty of freedom is in great part due to the creative diversity it engenders. The world would be much worse and less beautiful if everyone was just like you, or just like me.

There would be no game to play and there would be no life in any sense of the word if there were no proverbial cards out of your control dealt to accept and love as they are. You cannot play chess if all the pieces are the same color. You can not play cards if you get to choose all your own cards and all hands are equally infinitely easy to play. That would truly be the most lifeless world, one without cards out of your control, one without any diversity or challenge at all. Love the cards you are dealt. Love them all.

Love the people and the sunsets. Love the hungry lions and the frightened antelopes they chase. Love the day and night, and love the way the dark dances with the light.

Love isn't about owning, controlling, forcing, dominating, or even saving.

Generally, if you love something, you don't want to change it, control it, cage it, or own it.

You can sometimes help protect it from destruction, but in practice your supposed attempts to protect it will usually hurt or destroy it. You will usually kill the butterfly if you try to grasp it.

Usually, love means you just let go and admire. It is an unpossessive appreciation.

Conscious observation is what gives meaning and meaningful reality to the world you observe, whether you admire it or paint it as an unadmirable horror show. There is no observed world if there is no observer. You, *the real you*, give meaning to the world simply by observing it.

Admire that which you love. Don't try to grasp it. Just let go and admire. Let it be free. Let it be itself. Just let it be.

Sometimes the best way to help another human is simply to get out of their way.

Love typically isn't about doing anything. Love isn't about saving the world, or even necessarily changing the world—especially not this one tiny little planet.

It's about you, the real you, and how you look at the world.

Is it with judgment? With resentment? With clingy attachment?

Or is it with unconditional acceptance? Unpossessive appreciation? Overwhelming admiration? Graceful gratitude? Inner peace?

The Choice is Yours

A dream is real insofar as it is dreamt, at least that is insofar as it is consciously dreamt.

Your conscious experience of your experience provides reality and meaning to the experience.

I hope yours is a great one, a dream of inner peace, of triumph, of infinite grace.

As a dreamer of your dream, do you dream yourself as god of the dream or dream yourself as a faithful friend of god, perhaps a loyal servant? Or do you dream yourself as a character, an avatar, in a godless play, dramatic and eventful?

I think those are all beautiful dreams.

I have my dream too, but mine is no more right than yours, and yours no less right than mine. The beauty may be even more important than any rightness. I think in the eyes of the eternal, in the shared eyes of our mutual consciousnesses, the eternal reality would be worse if it lacked your dream, so I am thankful it doesn't.

I think it's perfect just the way it eternally is in the eternal now, where you and I are eternally one, yet beautifully diverse, each a god, each a friend, each a servant, each a master, each a dreamer, each a dream, each a player in a play, a playful play, an endless field, an eternal heaven in which we play together.

I love you, my friend, always, forever.

— I Love You —

You are quickly approaching the end of this book, but there is no monster at the end of this one.

Of this book, this is the final chapter. But your story has only just barely begun, a story that I hope is simultaneously filled with both exciting drama and constant underlying inner peace.

I imagine you would burst into tears if you even began to see the wonderful overwhelming possibilities that lay in front of you.

Whoever you are that reads this, I love you, truly.

These current human vessels of ours may have never met. These human lips of mine may never utter your human name.

Or we may have shared many laughs together.

We may have shared drinks together.

We may have had countless Nerf gun battles together, with many of the individual battles not even blasting off until after midnight.

We may have sparred until bloody, and even beyond, with boxing gloves in my backyard.

You may have literally choked me unconscious in jiu-jitsu class, resulting in a small memorable case of ironic amnesia for me.

We may have kicked over sixty-six garbage cans as teenagers, mentioned here with embarrassment not pride. Maybe a little pride. It's fun to be bad to the bone sometimes.

You may have been one of several police officers who have placed literal handcuffs on these wrists, even before these wrists had the tattoos they have now, the tattoo of my son's name on the left wrist—Tristen—and the tattoo of my daughter's name on the right wrist—Amaya.

You may have been a faceless companion a few cells down the line who chatted with me, by yelling down the hall, for hours to pass the time.

You may have been one of countless sages that I debated, using unnecessarily vivid verbosity, on internet philosophy forums, sometimes managing to get some bit of truth through my thick stubborn human skull.

You may have been one of countless childhood best friends with whom I have non-playfully fist-fought, only to be best friends again the next day, if not later the same day.

You may have been a friend's older brother, who would give me a nine-point handicap in a ten-point game of basketball and still almost always win, forced to suffer my boisterous gloating in the rare cases when I did manage to make one basket before you could make ten.

You may have been a family member who literally bailed me out of jail, which, perhaps sadly, is not a reference to one specific person or one specific incident.

You may have been a cool, calm, tough-looking upperclassman, who, at least from my childish eyes, seemed strangely intimidating, and who pulled over on the side of the road on a bitterly cold snowy day, without me asking or even imagining the possibility of such a thing; and while I was in the middle of walking home through the snow, you gave me a ride in a warm car with cool music and the seats reclined back to a degree I had never experienced before. At the time, I was only able to muster the two words, *"Thank you"*. After all these years, even if you read this now, you would almost certainly not realize these words are about you. I doubt the quick kind event was anywhere near as memorable for you as it was for me.

You may be a teacher or guidance counselor who attempted to persuade me to apply my alleged potential, or at least go to class, and when the time came to not drop out of school entirely. Though it may have seemed utterly unsuccessful in regard to the stated end, your care and attention were anything but unsuccessful. As young adults, teenagers really, just children in the grand scheme, it's well-known that we recklessly and arrogantly often feel all too invincible, drunk without drinking, but it's often forgotten that we also often feel all too invisible.

You may be a stranger on the street, passed with nothing more than a fleeting glance, or you may be a romantic partner with whom I've spent many passionate nights, pleasantly some nights and with very passionate arguing on some other days and some other nights. It may only be in a romantic context that I actually understand the words of the fictional character Seraph in the film series The Matrix, one of my favorites, who says, *"You do not truly know someone until you fight them."*

Whoever you are dear reader, I love you.

I wish you inner peace, unwavering confidence, and invincible endurance.

I wish you the salvation of grace, whatever that means for you, whether you find it in a church, find it in a temple, find it in a mosque, find it in a yoga studio, find it in a chair while reading this book, or find it mediating in your backyard. There is something great within you that can be found anywhere. Find it, if you haven't already. Find it again, if ever you lose sight of it, even for just a moment.

I wish you the spiritual strength and bravery to endure the fleeting emotional lows on the roller coaster of life. They are fleeting, so feel free to tell yourself in those times, *"This too shall pass."*

I wish you freedom from attachment and clingy possessiveness during the fleeting emotional highs on the roller coaster of life, so that you may truly enjoy the fleeting wonders with honest admiration and unpossessive love, not tainted with the fearful spiritual terror of greed, clinginess, or addiction. Though the addiction-prone flesh of these human vessels may encourage you otherwise, in those so-called good times, of so-called luck or wealth, I encourage you to also say to yourself, *"This too shall pass."*

It may be more of a metaphor to right now view your life *from above*, as the stoics often spoke of it, meaning to take perspective unbiased from the heat of the moment. Or one day you may literally find yourself on your literal deathbed moments away from certain death, contemplating your life, hopefully not distracted by such an utter cliché actually coming true for you.

If and when the time comes, literally or not, I hope you do joyfully realize the wonderful influence you have had.

In day-to-day practice, we often falsely see the world as filled with objects, solid things, be they moving or stationary, themselves props on a false Newtonian stage, a clockwork zombie world of objective unbending non-relative space and time. It can seem like a meaningless endless billiard ball game played by nobody.

But we know that's not how reality works. There are no such objects, and there is no such stage. And there is somebody.

What we misperceive as objects are wave-like ripples in an endless ocean, an ocean not of water but of possibility, an undrying and undying ocean that need not ever be replenished by rains.

Unlike finite objects on a mere Newtonian billiard-ball-like stage, in the vast seas in which we actually find ourselves, the ripples of even the tiniest transcendental pebble echo for all eternity, in the eternal now, echoing through both the would-be past and would-be future.

How different would this eternal ripple-filled present be without you? How different would this eternal world be without you?

Not without your body; let that remain in this hypothetical. Not without your would-be mere zombie brain; let that remain in this hypothetical. I am *not* asking how your human vessel without *you* fits into this beautiful puzzle of eternal reality. I am asking how your actual presence, the consciousness, meaning *you*, fits. How have you, *the real you*, changed things just by *being* here? Here in this eternal now we call reality? And by being here you've also in a manner of speaking been there for your human, so how have you changed things by being there for your human?

How might that human vessel have behaved differently if it wasn't conscious, truly conscious; if you, the real you, hadn't been there?

You are love. Not greedy possessiveness purporting itself as love, but real unpossessive divine beautiful love.

You are the source of inner peace.

If I was to speak of the Tao, the Truth, the Life, and the Light, you are the divine Light that illuminates the divine Truth.

You are the source of even the capacity for unconditional forgiveness and unconditional acceptance.

Yes, you are that love.

No unconscious zombie could experience the true glorious grace you have brought into this world. Would an unconscious zombie have even asked the questions about consciousness and reality that your experience of consciousness, its experience of you, has caused it to ask? Would a zombie have asked the questions, sometimes nonverbal, that it did contemplate because of you? Would a zombie have contemplated the nonverbal questions upon which one can meditate? Would a zombie version of your body have even meditated? Would a zombie version of your body have truly prayed in the most meaningful spiritual accepting graceful sense of the word *pray*? To truly pray, to meditate, to contemplate—this is part of your beautiful contribution to the fabric of reality.

There is a reason the word *temple* appears in the word *contemplate*. *Contemplate* comes from the Latin word *Templum*, which means temple. Your human body and would-be zombie brain may be a temple, but they wouldn't be without you.

You are the painter whose beautiful brush strokes ripple eternally in the diverse artwork that is the eternal present.

I love *you*.

Thank you for reading

Thank you for reading.

If you enjoyed this book, please do share it with someone.

Whatever your thoughts on what I have written, please do share them with me. You can email me your thoughts and comments at the following email address:

InItTogether@OnlineBookClub.org

I would be so happy to hear from you.

Gratitude to Street Team

I want to give special thanks to the street team who helped make this book possible:

- Hannah Compratt
- Sandra Nuttall
- Annmarie Hughes
- Heidi Simone
- Janaei Alexandria
- Robert Sterler
- David J Castello, author of *The Diary Of An Immortal (1945-1959)*
- Sunny Angel
- S. Jeyran Main